GREAT EDUCATORS
OF THREE CENTURIES

GREAT EDUCATORS

OF

THREE CENTURIES

THEIR WORK
AND ITS INFLUENCE ON MODERN EDUCATION

BY

FRANK PIERREPONT GRAVES

AMS PRESS
NEW YORK

Reprinted from the edition of 1912, New York
First AMS EDITION published 1971
Manufactured in the United States of America

International Standard Book Number: 0-404-02891-8

Library of Congress Number: 70-121285

AMS PRESS INC.
NEW YORK, N.Y. 10003

To My Colleagues and Friends
in the University of Missouri and
the Ohio State University
and among the Schoolmen
of Missouri and Ohio

PREFACE

It has now come to be understood that a series of essays upon the educational reformers cannot by any stretch of the imagination be termed a 'history of education.' The biographical and personal details must be subordinated and brought into perspective, and a suitable historical and philosophical connection given a work, before it can be so dignified. The present volume, therefore, is not intended to be a continuation of my *History of Education before the Middle Ages* and my treatment of the *Middle Ages and the Transition to Modern Times*. To a certain extent it duplicates material toward the end of the latter volume, and it largely anticipates my *History of Education in Modern Times*, but the nature and purpose of the present work are quite different.

I have felt that an account of the life and work of the men who, during the past three centuries, have introduced various innovations and reforms into modern education might contain interest and value for many who would never read a more comprehensive and unified production. I have, however, made some attempt as well to present the social setting of each reformer. Moreover, although the facts of biography are narrated somewhat at length, an effort has been made to eliminate everything that does not seem to have some bearing upon the contributions of the educator under consideration or upon the spread and permanence of his work. Such a treatment, I venture to hope, will prove of service to the general reader and to the student of educational origins whose time is limited. The volume may be used as a reference work, a reading circle book, or even as a text for classes that are not in condition to cope with the complexities of modern educational history. The worth of the book for any of these purposes has probably been heightened by a liberal quotation from the sources in the body of the text and the addition of supplementary readings at the end of each chapter.

This work is largely an outgrowth of my lectures before extension classes, teachers' institutes, and other informal gatherings in the states of Missouri and Ohio. I have, no doubt, unconsciously received much help from those who have listened to me upon these occasions, and have made bold to dedicate the book to them. More direct assistance, however, has been received from my friends, Professors Jesse H. Coursault of the University of Missouri, Arthur J. Jones of the University of Maine, and Edward O. Sisson of the University of Washington, and from my wife, Helen Wadsworth Graves.

F. P. G.

December 30, 1911.

CONTENTS

GREAT EDUCATORS OF THREE CENTURIES

CHAPTER I

JOHN MILTON AND HIS 'ACADEMY'

In the popular mind the name of *John Milton* (1608–1674) is associated only with the great epic, *Paradise Lost*. Scholars and literary men include a wider range of his poetry within their vision, and recognize a large difference between the products of his youthful period and those of his enriched maturity. But between these stages comes a period as a prose writer and pamphleteer, which, while little known even to the student of literature, has made Milton one of the interesting figures in education. The great poet was a stanch Puritan, and, during this middle stage of his career, several vigorous pamphlets of protest fell from his pen. He wrote upon the freedom of the press, the tenure of kings, religious toleration, and against the episcopacy. At this time, also, he undertook as part of his reforms to contribute to educational theory and to the improvement of the schools themselves. He conducted a boarding school throughout his thirties, and the *Tractate of Education*

Milton was a pamphleteer and a schoolmaster, as well as a poet, and wrote a *Tractate of Education*.

(1644) is an outgrowth of his practical experience as a schoolmaster.

Milton's Opposition to the Formal Humanism

His educational position is that of 'humanistic' and 'social realism,' which prepared the way for 'sense realism.'

Although he came somewhat later in the history of education, Milton is to be classed among those 'innovators'[1] who were endeavoring to introduce a broader humanism in the place of the narrow 'Ciceronianism' into which the educational product of the Renaissance had hardened. Instead of the restriction to words and set forms, they advocated a study of the ideas, or 'real things,' of which the words were the symbols. This emphasis upon the content of the classics, which has usually been known as 'humanistic' realism, is especially noticeable in Milton. With it often went the study of social and physical phenomena, in order to throw light upon the meaning of the passages under consideration. There seems also to have been an attempt to adapt education to actual living in a real world and to prepare young people for the concrete duties of life, and it was usually suggested that the breadth of view necessary for this could be obtained best through

---

[1] Other innovators were Rabelais, Montaigne, Mulcaster, etc. See Graves, *History of Education during the Transition*, Chap. XVII. Because of the nature of his educational position, Milton is treated here before Bacon, Ratich, and Comenius, although he follows them in point of time.

travel under the care of a tutor or by residence in a foreign school. This latter tendency, which appears to some extent in Milton's *Tractate*, may be called 'social' realism. However, while one element or the other may seem to be more prominent in a certain treatise, these two phases of education are largely bound up in each other, and both tendencies are evident in most reformers of the times. They seem to be but two sides of the same thing and to constitute together a natural bridge from the humanism of the later Renaissance to the 'sense realism' of the seventeenth century.

The *Tractate of Education* is an admirable illustration of this broader humanism. While a remarkable classicist himself, Milton objects to the usual humanistic education with its "grammatic flats and shallows where they stuck unreasonably to learn a few words with lamentable construction," and declares that the boys "do for the most part grow into hatred and contempt of learning." He claims that "we do amiss to spend seven or eight years in scraping together so much miserable Latin and Greek as might be learned otherwise easily and delightfully in one year." He especially stigmatizes, as Locke did later, the formal work in Latin composition, "forcing the empty wits of children to compose themes, verses, and orations, which are the acts of ripest judgment and the final work of a head filled by long reading and observing."

The *Tractate of Education* opposes the formal humanism.

His Encyclopædic but Humanistic Curriculum

and advocates ideas rather than words.

It is not, however, the study of classics in itself that Milton opposes, but the constant harping upon grammar without regard to the thought of the authors, for "though a linguist should pride himself to have all the tongues that Babel cleft the world into, yet if he have not studied the solid *things* [1] in them as well as the words and lexicons, he were nothing so much to be esteemed as any yeoman or tradesman competently wise in his mother dialect only." In this statement, as well as elsewhere, it is obvious that by 'things' Milton meant ideas and not objects.

Milton recommends an encyclopædic program, including sciences, but also a broad training in Latin and Greek,

Even in his recommendation of a most encyclopædic program of studies, which is usually one of the marks of the sense realist, he seems to imply the 'humanistic' rather than the 'sense' realism, although he wrote half a century after Bacon and was a younger contemporary of Comenius.[2] While his curriculum includes large elements of science and manual training, and especially emphasizes a knowledge of nature, it affords the broadest training in Latin and Greek, and, after the fashion of broader humanism in general, undertakes to teach agriculture through Latin, and natural history, geography, and medicine through Greek. On the whole,

[1] Italics not in the original.

[2] The *Tractate* is dedicated to Samuel Hartlib, who was also the friend and patron of Comenius, and a well-known sense realist. See footnote on page 2.

it is an education of books, and the enormous load of languages — Italian, Hebrew, Chaldee, and Syriac, as well as Latin and Greek, — together with mathematics, sciences, and other studies, would make such a course impossible, except, as some one has said, for a 'college of Miltons.'

His Broad Definition of Education

As with some of the other humanistic realists, notably Montaigne, Milton also would have considerable time given, toward the end of the course, to the social sciences, such as history, ethics, politics, economics, and theology, and to such practical training as would bring one in touch with life. He likewise advocates the experience and knowledge that would come from travel in England and abroad. Thus, in the place of the usual restricted conception of humanistic education, Milton would substitute a genuine study and understanding of the classical authors and a real preparation for life. While at first he piously declares that the aim of learning is "to repair the ruins of our first parents by regaining to know God aright," he is more specific later when he frames his famous definition : —

and much time on the social sciences, together with travel at home and abroad.

Hence he defines education from the standpoint of fitting one's environment.

"I call therefore a complete and generous education that which fits a man to perform justly, skilfully, and magnanimously all the offices both private and public of peace and war."

His Educational Institution, — the ' Academy '

The 'Academy' is to provide a secondary and higher education.

The school in which Milton would carry out his ideal education he calls an *Academy*, and states that it should be held in "a spatious house and ground about it, big enough to lodge one hundred and fifty persons." This institution should keep the boys from the age of twelve to twenty-one, and should provide both secondary and higher education, "not heeding a remove to any other house of scholarship, except it be some peculiar college of Law or Physic." And he adds: "After this pattern as many edifices may be converted to this use as shall be needful in every city throughout this land."

Influence of Milton's ' Academy ' in England and America

It was afterward adopted in a modified form by the nonconformists in England,

Strangely enough, this educational curriculum and organization of Milton's, exaggerated as they were, found a partial embodiment and function in a new educational institution that became of great importance in England and the United States. 'Academies' based upon this general plan were organized in many places to meet certain exigencies of the English nonconformists, that arose toward the end of Milton's life. The two thousand dissenting clergymen who were driven from their parishes by the harsh Act of Uniformity in 1662, in many instances found school-teaching a congenial means of

earning a livelihood, and at the same time of furnishing
higher education to the young dissenters who were excluded from the universities and 'grammar'[1] schools.
The first of these academies was that established by
Richard Frankland at Rathmill in 1665, and this was
followed by the institutions of John Woodhouse at
Sheriffhales, of Charles Morton at Newington Green,
and of some thirty other educators of whom we have
record. While these academies usually followed the
humanistic realism of Milton, and, since their chief function was to fit for the ministry, included Latin, Greek,
and Hebrew in their course, they were also rich in sciences, mathematics, and the social sciences, and the
vernacular was especially emphasized.[2] The new tendency was also broadened and amplified by the writings of Locke, whose *Thoughts*[3] became the great guide
for the managers of the Puritan academies. In 1689,
when the Act of Toleration put nonconformity upon a
legal footing, the academies were allowed to be regularly
incorporated.

So in America, when, by the middle of the eighteenth
century, the number of religious denominations had
greatly increased and the demands upon secondary

and for secondary education in America.

---

[1] See footnote on p. 8.

[2] A detailed account of the history and curriculum of these academies
is given in Brown, *Making of Our Middle Schools*, Chap. VIII.

[3] See pp. 52 ff.

education had expanded, the 'grammar' schools,[1] with their narrow denominational ideals and their limitation to a classical training and college preparation, proved inadequate, and an imitation of the English *academy* arose as a supplement. The first suggestion of an 'academy' was made in 1743 by Benjamin Franklin. He wished to inaugurate an education that would prepare for life, and not merely for college. He accordingly proposed for the youth of Pennsylvania a course in which English grammar and composition, penmanship, arithmetic, drawing, geography, history, the natural sciences, oratory, civics, and logic were to be emphasized. He would gladly have excluded the languages altogether and made the course completely realistic, but for politic reasons he made these subjects elective. His academy was opened at Philadelphia in 1751, and similar institutions sprang up rapidly through the other colonies during the latter half of the eighteenth century. Shortly after the Revolution, partly owing to the inability or the unwillingness of the towns or the counties to maintain grammar schools, the academy quite eclipsed these institutions, and became for a time the representative type of secondary school in the United States.[2]

[1] These 'grammar' schools were secondary institutions, and the classics composed the chief part of the curriculum. They had been borrowed from the (Latin) grammar schools of England by the American colonists. See Graves, *History of Education during the Transition*, pp. 172–174.   [2] See Brown, *op. cit.*, Chap. IX.

SUPPLEMENTARY READING

I. SOURCE

*MILTON, JOHN. *Tractate of Education.*

II. AUTHORITIES

*ADAMSON, J. W. *Pioneers of Modern Education.* Chap. VII.

BARNARD, H. *American Journal of Education.* Vol. II, pp. 61-76.

BARNARD, H. *English Pedagogy.* Pp. 145-190.

BROOKS, P. *Milton as an Educator* (in *Essays and Addresses,* pp. 300-319).

BROWNING, O. *History of Educational Theories.* Chap. VI.

*BROWNING, O. *Milton's Tractate of Education.*

*LAURIE, S. S. *Educational Opinion since the Renaissance.* Chap. XII.

LAURIE, S. S. *Essays and Addresses.* Chap. IX.

MASSON, D. *Life of Milton.* Vol. III, pp. 186-255.

*MORRIS, E. E. *Milton's Tractate of Education.* Introduction.

QUICK, R. H. *Educational Reformers.* Chap. XII, pp. 212-218.

* It is suggested that the general reader begin with the references marked with an asterisk. They are not necessarily the most valuable, but they are usually available and interesting.

CHAPTER II

FRANCIS BACON AND THE INDUCTIVE METHOD

'Sense realism' was a reflection of the scientific development in the sixteenth and seventeenth centuries. It led to new principles, content, method, and texts in education.

MILTON and other innovators represented realism in its early 'humanistic' and 'social' phases. But the realistic awakening did not cease with reviving the idea represented by the word or with the endeavor to bring the pupil in touch with the life he was to lead. The earlier or humanistic realism simply represents a stage in the process of transition from the narrow and formal humanism to the movement of sense realism. This later form of realism was a reflection of the great scientific development of the latter part of the sixteenth and the first half of the seventeenth centuries, with its variety of discoveries and inventions. The first great step in this movement was taken by Copernicus. Not until 1543 was his hypothesis of a solar system published, but as early as 1496 there had been a dissatisfaction with the existing Ptolemaic interpretation, and a groping after a more satisfactory explanation of the universe. After Copernicus, other great discoverers rapidly arose in Italy, France, Holland, and England, and the spirit of the new movement was felt in philosophy and education. Many new discoveries in science and inventions were made, and philosophy began to base itself upon reason and the senses. Kepler made it possible to search the heavens, Galileo reorganized the science of physics, and an air pump was invented by Guericke. This scientific progress was accompanied on the philosophic side by the rationalism of Descartes and the empiricism of Locke. The educational theorists, as a result, began to introduce science and a knowledge of real things into the curriculum. It was felt that humanism gave a knowledge only of words, books, and opinions, and did not even at its best lead to a study of real things. Hence new methods and new books were produced, to shorten and improve the study of the classical languages, and new content was imported into the courses of study. The movement would even seem to include some attempt at a formulation of scientific principles in education.

Bacon's New Method

The new tendency, however, did not appear in education until after the time of *Francis Bacon* (1561–1626). The use of the scientific method by the various discoverers was largely unconscious, and it remained for Bacon to formulate what he called the method of 'induction,' and, by advocating its use, to point the way to its development as a scientific theory of education. He is, therefore, ordinarily known as the first sense realist. Accord-

The scientific method was first formulated by Bacon, who, in opposition to the Aristotelian method, published his *Novum Organum*, by means of which he thought all

men might
attain
complete
knowledge
and truth.

ing to Dr. Rawley, his biographer, Bacon, while still at
the University of Cambridge, conceived a disgust for
Aristotle's philosophy as it was then taught. At any
rate, it is known that even during the busiest part of his
public career he undertook in sporadic works to combat
the Aristotelian method, and to form a new procedure
on the basis of the scientific discoveries of the day. Not
until 1620, however, did he publish his great treatise on
inductive reasoning called *Novum Organum* ('new instrument') in opposition to Aristotle's work on deduction. In behalf of his treatise Bacon argues that,
as the hand is helpless without the right tool to aid
it, so the human intellect is inefficient when it does not
possess its proper instrument or method, and, in his
opinion, all men are practically equal in attaining complete knowledge and truth, if they will but use the
mode of procedure that he describes. This new method
of seeking knowledge he contrasts with that in vogue,
as follows : —

"There are and can be only two ways of searching into and
discovering truth. The one flies from the senses and particulars
to the most general axioms, and from these principles, the truth
of which it takes for settled and immovable, proceeds to judgment and the discovery of middle axioms. And this way is now
in fashion. The other derives axioms from the senses and particulars, rising by a gradual and unbroken ascent, so that it arrives
at the most general axioms last of all. This is the true way, but
as yet untried."

Hence, Bacon would begin with particulars, rather than use the *a priori* reasoning of the syllogism, as advocated by the schoolmen under the impression that this was the method of Aristotle. Before, however, one's observations can be accurately made, Bacon felt it would be necessary to divest oneself of certain false and ill-defined notions to which humanity is liable. The preconceptions of which it is necessary to be rid are his famous 'idols.' These he declares to be of four classes: —

First, however, one must divest himself of certain preconceptions, or 'idols.'

"Idols of the Tribe, which have their foundation in human nature itself; Idols of the Cave, for every one, besides the faults he shares with his race, has a cave or den of his own; Idols of the Market-place, formed by the intercourse and association of men with each other; and Idols of the Theatre, which have immigrated into men's minds from the various dogmas of philosophies and also from wrong laws of demonstration."

Nor should the new method end with a mere collection of particulars. This proceeding Bacon believes to be useless and fully as dangerous for science as to generalize *a priori*, and holds that these two polar errors together account very largely for the ill success of science in the past. He declares: —

And one must not stop with particulars.

"Those who have handled sciences have been either men of experiment or men of dogmas. The men of experiment are like the ant; they only collect and use: the reasoners resemble spiders; who make cobwebs out of their substance. But the bee takes a middle course; it gathers its material from the flowers of the garden and the field, but transforms and digests it by a power of its own. Not unlike that is the true business of philosophy; for it neither relies solely or chiefly on the powers of the mind, nor does it take the matter which it gathers from natural history and mechanical experiments and lay it up in the memory whole, as it finds it; but lays it up in the understanding altered and digested. Therefore, from a closer and purer league between these two faculties, the experimental and the rational (such as has never yet been made), much may be hoped."

The facts must be tabulated and the 'forms' discovered.

In the second book of the *Novum Organum* Bacon begins, though he does not complete, a more definite statement of his method. Briefly stated, his plan was, after ridding the mind of its prepossessions, to tabulate carefully lists of all the facts of nature. It seemed to him a comparatively easy task to make, through the coöperation of scientific men, a complete accumulation of all the facts of science. After these data were secured, the next step would be to discover the ' forms ' of things, by which he means the underlying essence or law of each particular quality or simple nature. Such an abstraction could be achieved by a process of comparing the cases where the quality appears and where it does not appear, and of excluding the instances that fall under both heads until some 'form' is clearly present only when the quality is. Then, as a proof, another list may be drawn up where the quality appears in different degrees and where the 'form' should vary correspondingly.

'Salomon's House' and the Pansophic Course

A description of what Bacon thinks may be expected when this scientific method is systematically carried out can be found in his fable of the *New Atlantis*. The inhabitants of this mythical island are described as having in the course of ages created a state in which ideal sanitary, economic, political, and social conditions obtained. The most important institution of this society is its 'Salomon's House,' an organization in which the members devoted themselves to scientific research and invention, and in their supposed investigations Bacon anticipates much that scientists and inventors have to-day only just begun to realize. He represents these Utopian scientists as making all sorts of physical, chemical, astronomical, medical, and engineering experiments and discoveries, including the artificial production of metals, the forcing of plants, grafting, and variation of species, the infusion of serums, vivisection, telescopes, microphones, telephones, flying-machines, submarine boats, steam-engines, and perpetual-motion machines.

Bacon's idea of what may be accomplished by this new method is shown in his New Atlantis, where the members of 'Salomon's House' devote themselves to scientific research.

Bacon was not a teacher, and his treatment of educational problems appears in brief and scattered passages, and shows a failure to appreciate fully the importance to be attached to the education of the young.[1] Yet his

Education should be similarly organized on the basis of 'pansophia.'

[1] See *Advancement of Learning*, Bk. II, Chap. I; Bk. VI, Chap. IV; Bk. VII, Chap. III; also his essays, *Of Studies, Of Parents and Children, Of Custom and Education*, etc. While he would largely turn over the

description of 'Salomon's House' would seem to imply an interest in promoting scientific research and higher education at least, and a belief in such an organization of education that society might gradually accumulate a knowledge of nature and impart it to all pupils at every stage.   Perhaps this is attributing too much to the great English philosopher, but such certainly was the plan of Ratich and Comenius, who later on worked out the Baconian theory in education, and this dream of *pansophia* ('all-wisdom') formed part of the educational creed of the later realists in general.   Moreover, we know from the second book of his *Advancement of Learning* that Bacon ardently desired a reformation of the organization, content, and methods of higher education, and that among his suggestions for advancement were a wider course of study, more complete equipment for scientific investigation, a closer coöperation among institutions of learning, and a forwarding of the 'unfinished sciences.'

The Value of Bacon's Method

Bacon properly rejected the contemporary *a priori*

In estimating the method of Bacon, it is difficult to be fair.   The importance of his work has been as much exaggerated by some as it has been undervalued by others.

education of the young to the Jesuits, he is pedagogically wise in his suggestions as to the promotion of particular ability, the strengthening of mental weaknesses, and the methods of moral education.   See Sisson, *Francis Bacon on Education* (*Education*, November, 1908).

He reacted from the current view of Aristotle's reasoning, and, taking his cue from the many scientific workers of his time, formulated a new method in opposition to what he mistook as the position of the great logician. He very properly rejected the contemporary method of attempting to establish *a priori* the first principles of a science, and then deduce from them by means of the syllogism all the propositions which that science could contain. But in endeavoring to create a method whereby anyone could attain all the knowledge of which the human mind was capable, he undertook far too much. His effort to put all men on a level in reaching truth resulted in a most mechanical mode of procedure and neglected the part played by scientific imagination in the framing of hypotheses. Scientific method is not at present satisfied to hold, as Bacon did, that because all observed cases under certain conditions produce a particular effect, every other instance not yet observed will necessarily have the same property or effect. The modern procedure is rather that, when certain effects are observed, of which the cause or law is unknown, the scientist frames an hypothesis to account for them; then, by the process of deduction, tries this on the facts that he has collected; and if the hypothesis is verified, maintains that he has discovered the cause or law. Yet this is only a more explicit statement of what has always been implied in every process of reasoning. The method had certainly

method, but, in attempting to put all men on a level in attaining truth, he undertook too much, and made a most mechanical procedure.

c

been used by the later Greek philosophers, and it, as well as the syllogism, had even been formulated by Aristotle, although this part of his work was not known in Bacon's day.

Bacon cannot, therefore, really be said to have invented a new method   It is also evident that he failed to appreciate the work of Aristotle and the function of genius in scientific discovery.   But he did largely put an end to the existing process of *a priori* reasoning, and he did call attention to the necessity of careful experimentation and induction.   Probably no book ever made a greater revolution in modes of thinking or overthrew more prejudices than Bacon's *Novum Organum*.   It represents a culmination in the reaction that had been growing up through the Renaissance, the Reformation, and the earlier realism.

As far as education is concerned, Bacon, while not skilled or greatly interested in the work himself, influenced profoundly the writing and practice of many who were, and has done much to shape the spirit of modern education.   His method was first applied directly to education by a German known as Ratich, and, in a more effective way, by Comenius, a Moravian.

SUPPLEMENTARY READING

I. Source

*Bacon, F. *Philosophical Works* (edited by Spedding, Ellis and Heath).

II. Authorities

*Adamson, J. W. *Pioneers of Modern Education.* Chap. III.

Barnard, H. *American Journal of Education.* Vol. V, pp. 663–668.

Barnard, H. *English Pedagogy.* Pp. 77–122.

Beard, C. *The Reformation of the Sixteenth Century.* Chap. XI.

Caird, E. *University Addresses.* Pp. 124–156.

*Fowler, T. *Bacon's Novum Organum.*

Laurie, S. S. *History of Educational Opinion since the Renaissance.* Chap. X.

Munroe, J. P. *The Educational Ideal.* Chap. III.

Nichol, J. *Francis Bacon.*

Sisson, E. O. *Francis Bacon and the Modern University (Popular Science Monthly,* October, 1906) and *Francis Bacon on Education (Education,* November, 1908).

*Spedding, J. *Life and Times of Francis Bacon.*

CHAPTER III

RATICH AND HIS EDUCATIONAL CLAIMS

Ratich applied the Baconian method to the problems of education, especially language teaching.

Wolfgang von Ratke (1571–1635), generally called *Ratich* from an abbreviation of his Latinized name,[1] was born in Wilster, Holstein, and first studied for the ministry at the University of Rostock. Later, he continued his studies in England, where he probably became acquainted with the work of Bacon. Before long, realizing that he had an incurable defect in speech which would keep him from success in the pulpit, he decided to devote himself to educational reform. He planned to apply the principles of Bacon to the problems of education in general, but he intended especially to reform the methods of language teaching.

Ratich's Attempts at School Reform

In 1612 Ratich memorialized the imperial diet, while it was sitting at Frankfurt, and asked for an investigation of his methods. Two professors from the University of Giessen were commissioned to examine his propositions, and afterward the University of Jena similarly had four

---

[1] I.e. *Ratichius*.

of its staff look into the matter, and in each case a favor- able, not to say enthusiastic, verdict was reached.   When, however, on the strength of such reports, the town coun- cil of Augsburg gave him control of the schools of that city, he was not able to justify his claims, and the ar- rangement was abandoned at the end of a year.   Having appealed to the diet again without encouragement, Ratich began traveling from place to place, trying to interest various princes or cities in his system.   He was befriended by Dorothea, Duchess of Weimar, who in- duced her brother, Prince Ludwig of Anhalt-Köthen, to provide a school for Ratich.   This institution was fur- nished with an expensive equipment, including a large printing plant; a set of teachers that had been trained in the Ratichian methods and sworn to secrecy, were engaged; and some five hundred school children of Köthen were started on this royal road to learning.   The experiment lasted only eighteen months, and, largely owing to Ratich's inexperience as a schoolmaster, was a dismal failure.   The prince was so enraged at his pe- cuniary loss and the ridiculous light in which he was placed that he threw the unhappy reformer into prison, and released him at the end of three months only upon his signing a statement that he had undertaken more than he could perform.   After this, Ratich tried his hand at Magdeburg, where he failed again, mostly as the result of theological differences, and then was enabled to present his principles to Oxenstiern, the chancellor of Sweden, but he never really recovered from his disappointment in Köthen, and died of paralysis in Erfurt before he could hear from Stockholm.

His Claims and Methods

His claims concerning the teaching of languages, the arts and sciences, and uniformity, seem extravagant, but were in keeping with realism.

Although there was considerable merit in the principles of Ratich, he had many of the ear-marks of a mountebank. Such may be considered his constant attempts to keep his methods a profound secret, and the spectacular ways he had of presenting the ends they were bound to accomplish. In writing the diet, he promised by means of his system: first, to teach young or old Hebrew, Greek, and Latin without difficulty, and in a shorter time than was ordinarily devoted to any one language; secondly, to introduce schools in which all arts and sciences should be thoroughly taught and extended; and, lastly, to establish uniformity in speech, religion, and government. As Ratich stated them, these claims seemed decidedly extravagant, but as far as he expected to carry them out, they were but the natural aims of an education based upon realism and the Baconian method.

"First study the vernacular" and "one thing at

The rules of procedure used by Ratich and his disciples have been extracted by Von Raumer from a work on the Ratichian methods published after the system had become somewhat known.[1] In linguistic training he insisted, like all realists, that one "should first study the vernacular" as an introduction to other languages. He also held to the principle of "one thing at a time and often repeated." By this he meant that, in studying a language, one should master a single book. At Köthen, as soon as the children knew their letters, they were required to learn *Genesis* thoroughly for the sake of their German. Each chapter was read twice by the teacher, while the pupils followed the text with their finger. When they could read the book perfectly, they were taught grammar from it as a text. The teacher pointed out the various parts of speech and made the children find other examples, and then had them decline, conjugate and parse. In taking up Latin, a play of Terence was used in a similar fashion. A translation was read to the pupils several times before they were shown the original; then the Latin was translated to them from the text; next, the class was drilled in grammar; and finally, the boys were required to turn German sentences into Latin after the style of Terence. This method may have produced a high degree of concentration, but it was liable to result in monotony and want of interest, unless skilfully administered.

Another formulation of Ratich's, whereby he insisted

a time" were the principles upon which his practice at Köthen was based.

[1] *Methodus Institutionis Nova Ratichii et Ratichianorum*, published by Johannes Rhenius at Leipzig in 1626.

His other principles were similarly realistic.

upon "uniformity and harmony in all things," must have been of especial value in teaching the grammar of different languages, where the methods and even the terminology are often so diverse. Similarly, his idea that one should "learn first the thing and then its explanation," which was his way of advising that the details and exceptions be deferred until the entire outline of a subject is well in hand, would undoubtedly save a pupil from much confusion in acquiring a new language. And some of his other principles, which applied to education in general, are even more distinctly realistic. For example, he laid down the precept, "Follow the order of nature." Although his idea of 'nature' was rather hazy, and his methods often consisted in making fanciful analogies with natural phenomena, yet his injunction to make nature the guide seems to point the way to realism. Moreover, his attitude on "everything by experiment and induction," which completely repudiates all authority, went even farther and quite out-Baconed Bacon. And his additional recommendation that "nothing is to be learned by rote" looked in the same direction. Finally, these realistic methods were naturally accompanied by the humane injunction of "nothing by compulsion."

His Educational Influence

Thus Ratich not only helped shape some of the best methods for teaching languages, but he also anticipated many of the main principles of modern pedagogy. In carrying out his ideas, however, he was uniformly unsuccessful. This was somewhat due to his charlatan method of presentation, but more because of errors in his principles, his want of training and experience as a teacher, and the impatience, jealousy, and conservatism of others. He must have been regarded by his contemporaries in general as a complete failure, whenever they contrasted his promises with his performances. Nevertheless, it is clear that he stirred up considerable thought and had a wide influence. He won a great many converts to his principles, and, through the texts and treatises written as a result of the movement he stimulated, his ideas were largely perpetuated and expanded. In the next generation came Comenius, who carried out practically all the principles of Ratich more fully, and thus, in a way, the German innovator, unpractical as he was, became a sort of spiritual ancestor to Pestalozzi, Froebel, and Herbart.

Ratich anticipated much of modern pedagogy, although, because of charlatanism, inexperience, and the opposition of others, he failed to carry out his principles.

SUPPLEMENTARY READING

I. Source

RICHTER, A. *Ratichianische Studien* (Pts. 9 and 12 of *Neudrücke Pädagogischer Schriften*).

II. Authorities

*ADAMSON, J. W. *Pioneers of Modern Education.* Pp. 31–43.

BARNARD, H. *American Journal of Education.* Vol. V, pp. 229–256.

*BARNARD, H. *German Teachers and Educators.* Pp. 319–346.

BROWNING, O. *Educational Theories.* Chap. IV.

COMPAYRÉ, G. *History of Pedagogy.* Pp. 121–122.

*QUICK, R. H. *Educational Reformers.* Chap. IX.

CHAPTER IV

COMENIUS AND HIS GREAT DIDACTIC

Jan Amos Komensky (1592–1671), better known by his Latinized name of *Comenius*, was born at Nivnitz, a village of Moravia. He was, by religious inheritance, a devoted adherent of the Protestant sect called *Moravian Brethren*.[1] While he became bishop of the Moravians, and devoted many of his writings to religion or theological polemics, this does not concern us here, except as it affected his attitude as an educational reformer and a sense realist.

The Education and Earliest Work of Comenius

In his schooling, possibly as the result of careless guardianship of his inheritance, Comenius did not come to the study of Latin, the all-important subject in his day, until he was sixteen. This delay must,

Comenius was trained in a Latin school and at Herborn.

---

[1] The Moravian or Bohemian Church, officially known as *Unitas Fratrum*, is generally considered Lutheran in doctrine, but its religious descent goes back of Luther's time to the Bohemian martyr, Huss, and it has always preserved a separate organization. There are now three 'provinces' of Moravians, the German, British, and American. They number in all about thirty-five thousand members, of whom some twenty thousand are in the United States.

however, be regarded as most fortunate for education, as his maturity enabled him to perceive the amount of time then wasted upon grammatical complications and other absurdities in teaching languages, and was instrumental in causing him to undertake an improvement of method.   After his course in the Latin school, Comenius spent a couple of years in higher education at the Lutheran College of Herborn in the duchy of Nassau,[1] where he went to prepare for the ministry of his denomination, and

He then taught at Prerau and wrote his Easier Grammar.

at the University of Heidelberg.   Then, as he was still rather young for the cares of the pastorate, he taught for four years (1614–1618) in the school at Prerau, Moravia. Here he soon made his first attempt at simplifying the teaching of Latin by the production of a work called *Grammaticæ Facilioris Præcepta* ('Precepts of Easier Grammar').   Next (1618–1621) he became pastor at Fulneck.   Then, after a series of persecutions resulting from the Thirty Years' War, during which he and his fellow pastors were driven from pillar to post, he settled in 1627 at the Polish town of Leszno.[2]

The *Janua Linguarum* and Other Texts of the Series

In the Janua, the first of his remarkable

This place became the center from which most of his great contributions to education emanated.   During his

[1] The University of Prague, to which Comenius would naturally have gone, was at this time in the control of the Utraquists, a Hussite sect opposed to the Moravians.

[2] This town, now called *Lissa*, is a part of Prussia.

residence of fourteen years as rector of the Moravian series of texts on the study of Latin, he was influenced by Ratich and Bateus.
gymnasium here, he accomplished many reforms in the
schools, and began to embody his ideas in a series of
remarkable textbooks.   The first of these works was produced in 1631, and has generally been known by the name
of *Janua Linguarum Reserata* ('Gate of Languages Unlocked').   It was intended as an introductory book to
the study of Latin,[1] and consisted of an arrangement into
sentences of several thousand Latin words for the most
familiar objects and ideas.   The Latin was printed on
the right-hand side of the page, and on the left was given
a translation in the vernacular.   By this means the pupil
obtained a grasp of all ordinary knowledge and at the
same time a start in his Latin vocabulary.   In writing
this text, Comenius may have been somewhat influenced
by Ratich, the criticism of whose methods by the professors at Giessen [2] he had read while at Herborn,[3] but he
seems to have been more specifically indebted both for
his method and the felicitous name of his book to a
Jesuit known as Bateus,[4] who had written a similar work.

[1] In the first edition it was called *Janua Linguæ Latinæ Reserata*.

[2] See pp. 20 f.

[3] As, however, Ratich had failed to answer the letter of inquiry he wrote him from Leszno, Comenius must have largely worked out the plan independently.

[4] Batty or Bateus was an Irishman, although at the College of Sala-
manca in Spain. Comenius makes acknowledgments to him in the *Janua*, but says his ideas had been outlined some time before his attention was called to the book of the Jesuit father.

The *Vestibulum* was an introduction to the *Janua*; the *Atrium*, a third book; the *Palatium*, a fourth; the *Orbis Pictus*, an edition of the *Janua* with pictures; and the *Schola Ludus*, a dramatized *Janua*.

It was soon apparent that the *Janua* would be too difficult for beginners, and two years later Comenius issued his *Vestibulum* ('Vestibule') as an introduction to it. While the *Janua* contained all the ordinary words of the language, — some eight thousand, there were but a few hundred of the most common in the *Vestibulum*. Both of the works, however, were several times revised, modified, and enlarged. Also grammars, lexicons, and treatises to accompany them were written in later periods of Comenius's literary career. Much work of this sort was done between 1642 and 1650. During this period Comenius had accepted the invitation of Sweden to settle, under the patronage of his friend, Ludovic De Geer, at Elbing, a quiet town on the Baltic, and develop his ideas on method and school improvement. Here the *Vestibulum* and *Janua* were revised,[1] and the third of his Latin readers, the *Atrium* ('Entrance Hall'),[2] which took the pupil one stage beyond the *Janua*, was probably started. But the *Atrium* was not finished and published until Comenius began his residence of four years at Saros-Patak, where he was in 1650 urged by the prince of

[1] In Elbing the *Methodus Linguarum Novissima* ('Latest Method in Languages'), which outlines his idea of the purpose and principles of language teaching, together with several other didactic works, was also produced.

[2] When planning this work in the *Didactica Magna* (Chap. XXII, 19 and 22–24), he refers to it as *Palatium*, and the fourth book, afterward called *Palatium*, he there speaks of as *Thesaurus*.

Transylvania to come and reform the schools of the country.

From his description of an ideal school for Patak,[1] and from other works, it is known that he intended also to write a fourth [2] work in the Janual series, but he never completed it. This was to be known as *Sapientiæ Palatium* ('Palace of Wisdom'), and was to consist of selections from Cæsar, Sallust, Cicero, and others of the best prose writers. While in Patak, however, Comenius did write two supplementary textbooks, the *Orbis Sensualium Pictus* ('The World of Sense Objects Pictured') and the *Schola Ludus* ('School Plays'). The latter, which is an attempt to dramatize the *Janua*, soon fell into disuse, but the former, in which Comenius applied his principles of sense realism more fully than in any other of his readers, remained a very popular text for two centuries, and is most typical of the Comenian principles. It is practically an edition of the *Janua* accompanied with pictures, but is simpler and more extensive than the first issue of that book. Each object in a picture is marked with a number corresponding to one in the text.[3] It is the first illustrated reading book on record.

[1] *Scholæ Pansophicæ Delineatio.*

[2] It would be the fifth, if we should count the unimportant *Auctarium* ('Supplement'), which he afterward (1656) produced in Amsterdam and inserted between the *Vestibulum* and the *Janua.*

[3] The reprint of the English edition, published by Bardeen (Syracuse, 1887), should be consulted. This method of presentation is referred to by

The *Didactica Magna* as the Basis of All His Works

The *Didac-tica* gives his principles, organization, content, and methods of education.

Thus, throughout his life Comenius was more or less engaged at every period in writing texts for the study of Latin. But these books connected with method were only a part of the work he contemplated. During his whole career he had in mind a complete system of the principles of education, and of what, in consequence, he wished the organization, subject-matter, and methods to be. His ideas on the whole question of education were early formulated at Leszno in his *Didactica Magna* [1] ('Great Didactic'). While this work has many original features and is more carefully worked out than anything similar, Comenius frankly recognizes his obligations to many who have written previously. In fact, he rather strove to assimilate all that was good in the realistic movement and use it as a foundation. In this way the *Didactica* may be said to develop many of the scientific principles and methods found in Vives,[2] Bateus, Ratich,

It owes much to the works of Bacon, the *Encyclopædia* of Alsted, and the writings of many others.

Comenius as early as the *Vestibulum* as a desirable one, which at that time could not be carried out for lack of a skilful engraver. It may have been suggested to Comenius in the first instance by a Greek Testament edited early in the seventeenth century by a Professor Lubinus of the University of Rostock.

[1] This is a singular, the noun *ars* being understood. The original title has in it over one hundred words, beginning *Didactica Magna; Omnes Omnia Docendi Exhibens*. For a translation of the entire title, see Keatinge, *The Great Didactic of Comenius*, p. 155.

[2] *Juan Luis Vives* (1492–1540) was a Spanish humanist, who spent

Andreæ,[1] Frey,[2] and Bodinus,[3] but it owes a greater debt for its pansophic basis of education to the works of Bacon and even more to the *Encyclopædia* of Johann Heinrich Alsted, under whom Comenius had studied at Herborn. The *Didactica* seems to have been completed in the Moravian dialect[4] about the time the *Janua* first appeared, and must have been contemplated somewhat earlier. Hence, while this work was not translated into Latin and published until 1657, and was never printed in the language in which it was originally written until a century and three quarters after the death of its author, the point of view must have been established even before Comenius came to Leszno, and influenced him throughout his career.

The rest of the books of Comenius may be regarded as amplifications of certain parts of the *Didactica*. To make his instructions on infant training more explicit, he wrote, while still at Leszno, the *Informatorium Skoly*

The *Didactica* was made explicit in the *Mother School*, the vernacular

several years in England. His chief treatise, *De Tradendis Disciplinis*, insists upon religion and classics as the main content of education.

[1] *Johann Valentin Andreæ* (1586–1654), court preacher at Stuttgart, attacked the formal religion and education of the times in numerous pamphlets.

[2] *Janus Cæcilius Frey* (?–1631) was a German educationalist, living in Paris, who produced a number of practical works.

[3] *Jean Bodin* (1530–1596) was a French writer on political theory, who published also an unusual educational treatise called *Methodus ad facilem historiarum cognitionem*.

[4] *Czech* was spoken in Moravia.

D

Materske ('Handbook of the Mother School').[1]   He also supplemented the *Didactica* with a set of texts for the 'vernacular school' similar to the Janual series, which were intended for the 'Latin School'; but, being written in an obscure dialect, these vernacular works were never revised and soon disappeared.[2]   But the phase of the *Didactica* most often elaborated both in his other works and in his school organization was the realistic one of *pansophia* ('universal knowledge'). This was most manifest in his desire to teach at least the rudiments of all things to every one.   It has already been seen how this principle has been emphasized in his textbooks, such as the *Janua* and the *Orbis Pictus*.   Also, after producing treatises upon *Astronomy* and *Physics*, he wrote, while at Leszno and Elbing, several works specifically on *pansophia*, of which the *Janua Rerum Reserata* ('Gate of Things Unlocked') is the most systematic and complete. These works, while diluted by traditional conceptions but little beyond those of scholasticism,[3] show how far

(margin notes:) series, and the Janual series.

(margin notes:) Attempts of Comenius at 'pansophia.'

---

[1] This work was written first in Czech, although not published in that dialect for two centuries and a quarter.   It was issued in German in 1633, and in Latin in 1657.   Will S. Monroe has translated the Latin edition into English under the title of *The School of Infancy* (Boston, 1896).

[2] The names of these texts, as he gives them in his *Scholæ Vernaculæ Delineatio*, were *Violarium* ('Violet-bed'), *Rosarium* ('Rose-bed'), *Viridarium* ('Grass-plot'), *Labyrinthus* ('Labyrinth'), *Balsamentum* ('Balsam-bed'), and *Paradisus Animæ* ('Paradise of the Soul').   Cf. also the *Didactica*, Chap. XXIX, II.

[3] For example, with Comenius the constituents of the universe are reduced to matter, spirit, and light.

Comenius, by organizing his data about large principles, instead of merely accumulating facts, had advanced beyond previous attempts. Further, in his *Didactica* he recommends that a great College of Pansophy, or scientific research,[1] be established, and in 1641, just before his call to Sweden, he went to England, at the invitation of Parliament, to start an institution of this character there. At Patak he even undertook to establish a pansophic school of secondary grade, as outlined in his *Pansophicæ Scholæ Delineatio* ('Plan of a Pansophic School').

Pansophia as His Ruling Passion

This idea of *pansophia* seems to have been most keen and vivid with Comenius all his life, but he was always prevented from undertaking it to any extent by one accident or another, and was doomed to constant disappointment. Finally, shortly after his return from Patak, when Leszno was burned by the Poles,[2] Comenius barely escaped with his life, and his *silva*, or collection of pansophic materials, upon which he had worked for forty years,

His pansophic materials were burned at Leszno.

---

[1] He calls it a *collegium didacticum*.

[2] The Moravians, who had suffered so severely from the Catholics during the Thirty Years' War, were in secret sympathy with the Protestant Swedes during their invasion of Poland. After the peace was declared, and several towns, including Leszno, were ceded to Sweden, Comenius foolishly published a letter of congratulation to the Swedish king, Charles Gustavus, and, in retaliation, the Poles attacked Leszno and plundered it.

was completely destroyed. He was now in his sixty-fifth year and had not the strength or courage to pursue his favorite conception further.

The Threefold Aim of Education

According to Comenius, education should aim at knowledge, morality, and piety.

While mystic and narrow at times, Comenius was a sincere Christian, and his view of life is most consistently carried out in his conception of education. He hoped for a complete regeneration of mankind through an embodiment of religion in the purpose of education. This educational aim is shown in the following propositions, which he develops in successive chapters of the *Didactica:* —

"(I) Man is the highest, the most absolute, and the most excellent of things created; (II) the ultimate end of man is beyond this life; (III) this life is but a preparation for eternity; (IV) there are three stages in the preparation for eternity: to know oneself (and with oneself all things), to rule oneself, and to direct oneself to God;[1] (V) the seeds of these three (learning, virtue, religion[2]) are naturally implanted in us; (VI) if a man is to be produced, it is necessary that he be formed by education."

Man's lower nature should

Thus, from his religious conception of society, Comenius works out as his aim of education *knowledge, morality,*

---

[1] In the original, *Se et secum omnia, Nosse; Regere; et ad Deum Dirigere.* Cf.

"Self-reverence, self-knowledge, self-control, —
These three alone lead life to sovereign power."
— TENNYSON'S *Œnone.*

[2] I.e. *eruditio, virtus seu mores honestas, religio seu pietas.*

and piety, and makes these ideals go hand in hand. It
is to be noted, however, that his ideas about what constitutes religion have advanced a long way beyond those
of mediæval times. He regards education not as a means
of ridding oneself of all natural instincts, and of exalting
the soul by degrading the body, but as a system for con-
trolling the lower nature by the higher through a mental,
moral, and religious training. Education should enable
one to become pious through the establishment of moral
habits, which are in turn to be formed and guided through
adequate knowledge.

be controlled by the higher.

Universal Education and the Four School Periods

But as with Comenius education is to prepare us to
live as human beings, rather than to fit us for station,
rank, or occupation, he further holds: —

There should be one system of schools for all.

"(VIII) The young must be educated in common, and for
this schools are necessary; (IX) all the young of both sexes should
be sent to school."

Under these headings he shows that, while the parents
are responsible for the education of their children, it has
been necessary to set aside a special class of people for
teachers and to create a special institution known as the
school, and that there should be one system of schools
for all alike, — "boys and girls, both noble and ignoble,
rich and poor, in all cities and towns, villages and ham-
lets."

The 'school
of the moth-
er's lap,' the
'vernacular
school,' the
'Latin
school,' and
the 'acad-
emy.'

Later on,[1] the *Didactica* more fully describes the organization that Comenius believes would be most effective.   The system should consist of four periods of six
years each, ranging from birth to manhood.   The first
period of instruction is that through infancy, which lasts
up to the age of six, and the school is that of the 'mother's
lap.'[2]   Next comes childhood, which continues until the
pupil is twelve, and for this is to be organized the 'vernacular,' or elementary, school.   From that time up to
eighteen comes the period of adolescence, with its 'Latin,'
or secondary, school.   Finally, during youth, from eighteen to twenty-four, the 'academy,' or university, together with travel, should be the means of education.
As to the distribution and scope of these institutions,
Comenius declares: —

"A mother school should exist in every house, a vernacular
school in every hamlet and village, a Latin school in every city,
and a university in every kingdom or in every province.   The
mother school and the vernacular school embrace all the young
of both sexes.   The Latin school gives a more thorough education
to those who aspire higher than the workshop; while the university trains up the teachers and learned men of the future, that
our churches, schools, and states may never lack suitable leaders."

Hence only those of the greatest ability, 'the flower of
mankind,' were to go to the university.   "A public

[1] Chaps. XXVII–XXXI.
[2] This was known as *Schola Materni Gremii* in the Latin version.

examination should be held for the students who leave the Latin school, and from its results the masters may decide which of them should be sent to the university and which should enter the other occupations of life. Those who are selected will pursue their studies, some choosing theology, some politics, and some medicine, in accordance with their natural inclination, and with the needs of the Church and of the State."

Such an organization of schools as that suggested by Comenius would tend to bring about the custom of educating according to ability, rather than social status, and would thus enable any people to secure the benefit of all their genius. It was a genuine 'ladder' system of education, open to all, and leading from the kindergarten through the university, such as has been commended by Huxley in speaking of the American schools. At the day that Comenius proposed it, this organization was some three centuries in advance of the times. Such an idea of equal opportunities for all could have been possible in the seventeenth century only as the educational outgrowth of a religious attitude like that of Comenius, and may well have been promoted in his case by the simple, democratic spirit of the little band of Christians whose leader he was.[1]

A 'ladder' system of education.

[1] In the old cemeteries of the Moravian communities of the United States, the departed lie side by side without distinction in regard to position, wealth, or color. The tombstones are laid flat upon the graves,

The Pansophic College and the Encyclopædic Courses of Study

A coöperative college of investigation known as a 'Schola Scholarum.'

But beyond the university, which, like the lower schools, was to make teaching its chief function, Comenius held it to be important that somewhere in the world there should be a *Schola Scholarum* or *Collegium Didacticum*, which should be devoted to scientific investigation. Through this pansophic college, learned men from all nations might coöperate, and, he holds, —

"These men should . . . spread the light of wisdom throughout the human race with greater success than has hitherto been attained, and benefit humanity by new and useful inventions. For this no single man and no single generation is sufficient, and it is therefore essential that the work be carried on by many, working together and employing the researches of their predecessors as a starting-point."

This pansophic college was to form a logical climax to the system of schools.

This plan of a 'Universal College' for research would seem to be a natural product of the pansophic ideal, which has been seen [1] to dominate all of the educational theory of Comenius. Such an institution would form a logical climax to his system of schools, bearing, as he says, the same relation to them that the stomach does to the other members of the body by "supplying blood, life, and

and are exactly alike, except for size, so that none in this Christian family may appear more prominent than the other. A similar interpretation of the Master's 'brotherhood of man' is evidenced in all the Moravian social life.   [1] See pp. 35 f.

strength to all," for he holds that a training in all subjects should be given at every stage of education. Such universal knowledge, however, Comenius believes, should be given only in outline at first, and then more and more elaborately and thoroughly as education proceeds. The *Didactica*, accordingly, states : —

"These different schools are not to deal with different subjects, but should treat the same subjects in different ways, giving instruction in all that can produce true men, true Christians, and true scholars; throughout graduating the instruction to the age of the pupil and the knowledge that he already possesses. . . . In the earlier schools everything is taught in a general and undefined manner, while in those that follow the information is particularized and exact; just as a tree puts forth more branches and shoots each successive year, and grows stronger and more fruitful." [1]

In later chapters of the *Didactica* and in his works for the special stages, Comenius gives the details of the pansophic training in each period of education. Even in the mother school, it is expected that the infant shall be taught geography, history, and various sciences; grammar, rhetoric, and dialectic; music, arithmetic, geometry, and astronomy; and the rudiments of economics, politics, ethics, metaphysics, and religion; as well as encouraged in sports and the construction of buildings. The attainment at this stage is, of course, not expected

Even the course in the mother school is to be pansophic.

[1] Chap. XXVII, 4–5. This is practically the modern German method of teaching, known as that of 'concentric circles.'

to be as formidable as the names of the subjects sound. It is to consist merely in understanding simple causal, temporal, spatial, and numerical relations; in distinguishing sun, moon, and stars, hills, valleys, lakes, and rivers, and animals and plants; in learning to express oneself, and in acquiring proper habits. It is, in fact, very much like the training of the modern kindergarten.

So the vernacular school is to afford instruction in all subjects, in case the pupil can go no further.

Similarly, the vernacular school is to afford more advanced instruction in all literature, morals, and religion that will be of value throughout life, in case the pupil can go no further. The course is to include, beside the elements, morals, religion, and music, everyday civil government and economics, history and geography, with especial reference to the pupil's own country, and a general knowledge of the mechanic arts. All these studies are to be given in the native tongue, since it would take too long to acquire the Latin, and those who are to go on will learn Latin more readily for having a wide knowledge of things to which they have simply to apply new names instead of those of the vernacular.

The Latin school offers four languages, but continues this encyclopædic training.

The Latin school, while including four languages, — the vernacular, Latin, Greek, and Hebrew, is also to continue this encyclopædic training. The seven liberal arts are to be taught in more formal fashion, and considerable work is to be given in physics, geography, chronology, history, ethics, and theology. In his description of the pansophic school that he undertook to establish at Patak,

Comenius gives an even more specific account of the range of knowledge that should be gained in secondary education. He maps out seven classes, of which the first three are to be called 'philological,' and the other four to be known as 'philosophical,' 'logical,' 'political,' and 'theological,' respectively. In the philological grades, he indicates that Latin is to be taught; arithmetic, plane and solid geometry, and music are to be gradually acquired; and instruction is to be afforded in morality, the catechism, the Scriptures, and psalms, hymns, and prayers. So he gives exactly the amount of training in mathematics, the arts and sciences, and religion that is to appear in the next three classes, and arranges that Greek shall be studied and Hebrew begun. In the last class, the wide range of secular knowledge is to be continued, and such theological matters as the relation of souls to God are to be discussed.

Finally, in the case of the university, Comenius maintains that "the curriculum should be really universal, and provision should be made for the study of every branch of human knowledge," but "each student should devote his undivided energies to that subject for which he is evidently suited by nature," — theology, medicine, law, music, poetry, or oratory. However, "those of quite exceptional talent should be urged to pursue all the branches of study, that there may always be some men whose knowledge is encyclopædic."

In the university each student should devote himself to a specialty, but a few should pursue all branches.

The Method of Nature

Thus at every stage of education Comenius believes that there should be pansophic instruction. The way in which this knowledge is to be acquired, he intends also to have in full accord with sense realism. He insists that, in order to reform the schools of the day, which were uninteresting, wasteful of time, and cruel, the 'method of nature' must be observed and followed, for "if we wish to find a remedy for the defects of Nature, it is in Nature herself that we must look for it, since it is certain that art can do nothing unless it imitate Nature." He then shows how Nature accomplishes all things "with certainty, ease, and thoroughness," [1] in what respects the schools have deviated from the principles of nature, and how they can be rectified only by following her plans.

One should follow the 'method of nature,' which accomplishes all things "with certainty, ease, and thoroughness."

These principles concerning the working of nature were, however, not established inductively by Comenius, but laid down *a priori*, and were mostly superficial and fanciful analogies. The following quotation from the *First Principle* that he gives under the 'certainty' of nature, may serve as a specimen of his method: —

The analogy of the bird.

"*Nature observes a suitable time*. For example, a bird that wishes to multiply its species, does not set about it in winter, when everything is stiff with cold, nor in summer, when everything is parched and withered with heat; nor yet in autumn, when the vital force of all creatures declines with the sun's declin-

---

[1] I.e. *certo, facile, solide*. See *Didactica*, Chap. XIV–XVIII.

ing rays, and a new winter with hostile mien is approaching; but in spring, when the sun brings back life and strength to all."

The schools deviate from this method of nature, he claims in the first place, because "the right time for mental exercise is not chosen," and to rectify the error, —

"(I) The education of men should be commenced in the spring-time of life, that is to say, in boyhood (for boyhood is the equivalent of spring, youth of summer, manhood of autumn, and old age of winter). (II) The morning hours are the most suitable for study, for here again the morning is the equivalent of spring, midday of summer, the evening of autumn, and the night of winter."

It is not remarkable that, with all his realistic tendencies, Comenius did not employ the inductive method to any extent. He had inherited the notion that not all truth can be secured through the senses or by reason. He claimed that even Bacon's method could not be applied to the entire universe, all of which is included in his *pansophia*. There are, he held, three media for knowledge, — the senses, the intellect, and revelation, and "error will cease if the balance between them is preserved." The natural sciences were young in the day of Comenius, and he was very limited in his grasp of their content and method. It is a sufficient merit that, imbibing the spirit of sense realism, he had for the first time in history applied anything like induction to teaching, and produced the most systematic and

The inductive method was not employed to any extent.

thorough work upon educational method that had been known.

How the principles for following nature may be made effective; the application of the general method to the sciences, arts, languages, morality, and piety.

After working out in the *Didactica* these general principles for following nature, Comenius renders his work much more practical by showing how such principles may be made effective in the ordinary schools. He then applies his general method to the specific teaching of various branches of knowledge, — sciences, arts (including reading, writing, singing, composition, and logic), and languages, and to instruction in morality and piety. On this practical side of his method, he applies more fully the induction of Bacon. After showing the necessity for careful observation in obtaining a knowledge of the sciences, he gives nine useful precepts for their study, and while they are stated as general principles, they are clearly the inductive result of his own experience as a teacher. Similarly he formulates rules for instruction in the arts, languages, morality, and piety. The description of special method in sciences, too, is thoroughly in harmony with realism in its insistence that, in order to make a genuine impression upon the mind, one must deal with realities rather than books. The objects themselves, or, where this is not possible, such representations of them as can be conveyed by copies,

Impression must be insured by expression.

models, and pictures, must be studied. In the case of the languages, arts, morality, and piety, impression must be insured by expression. "What has to be done, must be learned by doing." Reading, writing, and singing are to be acquired by practice. The use of foreign languages affords a better means of learning them than do the rules of grammar. Practice, good example, and sympathetic guidance teach us virtue better than do precepts. Piety is instilled by meditation, prayer, and self-examination.

As would be expected from the threefold interrelated aim and the encyclopædic content of education, Comenius everywhere in his method intends that all subjects shall be correlated. In particular, he holds: — *The study of languages to be correlated with that of objects.*

"The study of languages, especially in youth, should be joined to that of objects, that our acquaintance with the objective world and with language, that is to say, our knowledge of facts and our power to express them, may progress side by side." [1]

In the matter of discipline, as a natural accompaniment of his improvements in method, Comenius was in advance of his time. He holds that the end of discipline is to prevent a recurrence of the fault, and it must be inflicted in such a way that the pupil will recognize that it is for his own good. Severe punishment must not be administered for a failure in studies, but only for a moral breach, and exhortation and reproof are to be used before resorting to more stringent measures. *Discipline should be administered only for a moral breach.*

[1] This principle, it has been seen (pp. 28 ff.), Comenius carried out in his series of Latin textbooks.

The Influence of Comenius upon Education

To sense realism Comenius added the endowment of piety.

Such was the work of Comenius, who may in the fullest sense be considered a great educational reformer and the real progenitor of modern education. His position grew out of sense realism, but to the encyclopædic content and the natural method of Bacon, Ratich, and others, which he rendered more elaborate, consistent, and rational, he added his natural endowment of innate piety and a sense of the 'brotherhood of man.' Comenius made it evident that education should be a natural, not an artificial and traditional, process in harmony with man's very constitution and destiny, and that a well-rounded training for complete living should be everywhere afforded to all, without regard to sex, social position, or wealth, because of their very humanity. He outlined a regular system of schools and described their grading, and was the first to suggest a training for very young children. He held that bodily vigor and physical education were essential, and made sense training an important part of the course. He further broadened and enriched the entire curriculum by subordinating Latin to the vernacular, and insisting upon geography, history, the elements of all arts and sciences, and such other studies as would fit one for the activities of life. He correlated and coördinated all subjects, and combined even the training in Latin with a knowledge of

Education should be in harmony with one's nature, and should be universal.

Physical education and sense training should be part of the course.

All subjects should be correlated.

real things. This he accomplished through a series of textbooks that were a great advance over anything previously produced. Thus he greatly contributed to make education more effective, interesting, pleasant, and natural.

However, for nearly two centuries Comenius had but little direct effect upon the schools, except for his language methods and his texts. The *Janua* was translated into a dozen European, and at least three Asiatic, languages; the *Orbis Pictus* proved even more popular, and went through an almost unlimited number of editions in various tongues; and the whole series became for many generations the favorite means of introducing young people to the study of Latin. But until about half a century ago, the work of Comenius as a whole had purely an historical interest, and was known almost solely through the *Orbis Pictus*. The great reformer was viewed as a fanatic, especially as the pansophic ideal turned out to be of only ephemeral interest. Humanism was too thoroughly intrenched to give way at once to realism.

Comenius had little influence upon schools, except through his language texts,

Nevertheless, the principles of Comenius were unconsciously taken up by others and have become the basis of modern education. Francke was anticipated by Comenius in suggesting a curriculum that would fit one for life; before Rousseau, Comenius intimated that the school system should be adapted to the child rather than

but his principles have become the basis of modern education, and have influenced Francke, Rousseau,

E

the child to the system; Basedow largely modeled his encyclopædic content and natural method after the *Orbis Pictus;* Pestalozzi revived the universal education, love of the child, and object teaching that appear in the works of the old bishop; Herbart's emphasis upon character and upon scientific method and curriculum seem like an echo of Comenius; while the kindergarten, 'self-activity,' and play, suggested by Froebel, had been previously outlined by the Moravian. Hence it happened that in the middle of the nineteenth century, when the works of Comenius were once more brought to light by German investigators, it was discovered that the old realist of the seventeenth century had been the first to deal with education in a scientific spirit, and work out its problems practically in the schools. His evidently was the clearest of visions and broadest of intellects. While it is easy to criticize him now, in the light of history Comenius is a most important individual in the development of modern education.

SUPPLEMENTARY READING

I. SOURCES

*COMENIUS, J. A.   *Great Didactic* (translated by M. W. Keatinge), *Orbis Pictus* (reprint of C. W. Bardeen), and *School of Infancy* (translated by W. S. Monroe).

II. AUTHORITIES

ADAMSON, J. W.   *Pioneers of Modern Education.*   Chaps. III–V.

BARNARD, H.   *American Journal of Education.*   Vol. V, pp. 257–298.

BARNARD, H.   *German Teachers and Educators.*   Pp. 347–388.

BROWNING, O.   *Educational Theories.*   Chap. IV.

*BUTLER, N. M.   *The Place of Comenius in the History of Education.*

COMPAYRÉ, G.   *History of Pedagogy.*   Pp. 122–137.

DAVIDSON, T.   *History of Education.*   Pp. 193–197.

*HANUS, P. H.   *The Permanent Influence of Comenius.*   (*Educational Aims and Values,* VIII.)

LAURIE, S. S.   *Educational Opinion since the Renaissance.*   Chap. II.

*LAURIE, S. S.   *John Amos Comenius.*

*MONROE, W. S.   *Comenius and the Beginnings of Educational Reform.*

MUNROE, J. P.   *The Educational Ideal.*   Chap. IV.

*QUICK, R. H.   *Educational Reformers.*   Chap. X.

CHAPTER V

JOHN LOCKE AND EDUCATION AS DISCIPLINE

Locke's theories should be estimated by his Conduct of the Understanding, rather than by his Thoughts concerning Education.

THE educational position of *John Locke* (1632–1704) is usually misinterpreted. The general estimate of his theory is taken from his work entitled *Some Thoughts concerning Education*. This treatise grew out of his experience as a private tutor in the family of the Earl of Shaftesbury, and consists of a set of practical suggestions for the education of a gentleman, rather than a scholar. The recommendations contained in the *Thoughts* are consequently somewhat at variance with the underlying principles of Locke's philosophy, as given in his famous *Essay concerning the Human Understanding*, and with the intellectual training suggested in his other educational work, *Conduct of the Understanding*, which was originally an additional book and an application of the *Essay*.

Locke as a 'Humanistic'-'Social' Realist

In the Thoughts he appears to be mainly a 'humanistic'-'social' realist.

If the *Thoughts* alone is read, Locke will naturally be considered in the main a 'humanistic'-'social' realist, like Montaigne, but also as leaning somewhat toward the 'sense realism' of Comenius. Like Montaigne,

52

Locke holds that book education and intellectual training are of less importance than the development of character and polish. After treating bodily education at considerable length, he states the aims of education in the order of their value as "*Virtue, Wisdom (i.e.* worldly wisdom), *Breeding,* and *Learning,*" and later adds: —

"Learning must be had, but in the second place, as subservient only to greater Qualities. Seek out somebody that may know how discreetly to frame his Manners: Place him in Hands where you may, as much as possible, secure his Innocence, cherish and nurse up the good, and gently correct and weed out any bad Inclinations, and settle in him good Habits. This is the main Point, and this provided for, Learning may be had into the Bargain." *Character is made of the first importance in education.*

Such a training, Locke agrees with Montaigne, can be secured only through personal attention, and the young gentleman should be given a tutor when his father cannot properly look after his training. Likewise, he feels that, "to form a young Gentleman as he should be, 'tis fit his *Governor* should himself be well-bred, understanding the Ways of Carriage and Measures of Civility in all the variety of Persons, Times, and Places; and keep his Pupil, as much as his Age requires, constantly to the Observation of them." This private training is infinitely to be preferred, Locke holds, to that "from such a troop of Play-fellows as schools usually assemble from Parents of all kinds." Locke also believes, with Mon- *The proper training comes through a tutor rather than schools.*

Travel at the right time.

taigne and Milton, in foreign travel as a means of broad education and adaptation to living. He thinks, however, that it should not, as it usually did, come at the critical period between sixteen and twenty-one, but either earlier, when the boy is better able to learn foreign languages, or later, when he can intelligently observe the laws and customs of other countries.

Locke is opposed to the narrow humanism, but thinks Latin necessary to a gentleman, and that it should be learned by speaking.

Locke approaches the earlier realists even more closely in showing scant respect for the narrow humanism and tedious methods of the grammar school. He declares specifically : —

"When I consider what an ado is made about a little *Latin* and *Greek*, how many Years are spent in it, and what a Noise and Business it makes to no purpose, I can hardly forbear thinking that the Parents of children still live in Fear of the Schoolmaster's Rod, which they look on as the only Instrument of Education; as a language or two to be its whole Business."

Yet Locke agrees with Montaigne again in thinking that Latin is, after all, "absolutely necessary to a Gentleman," but that "'tis a Wonder Parents, when they have had the Experience in French, should not think (it) ought to be learned the same way, by talking and reading," [1] instead of through grammar, theme writing, versification, and memorizing long passages. Greek, however, Locke does not regard as essential to a gentleman's edu-

[1] When conversation is impossible, he recommends the use of interlinear translations.

cation, although he may in manhood take it up by himself.

As a further part of 'intellectual education,' Locke holds that, "besides what is to be had from Study and Books, there are other *Accomplishments* necessary for a Gentleman," — dancing, horseback riding, fencing, and wrestling. The pupil should also, he contends, "*learn a Trade, a manual Trade;* nay, two or three, but one more particularly." This the future gentleman should acquire, not with the idea of ever engaging in it, but for the sake of health and of "easing the wearied Part by Change of Business." [1]

Dancing, horseback riding, fencing, wrestling, and a trade.

Locke as a 'Sense Realist'

But there are also elements throughout the *Thoughts* and to some extent in the *Conduct*, where Locke seems to have been affected by the concrete material and interesting methods of Comenius, the great 'sense' realist, as clearly as he was elsewhere by the earlier realism of Montaigne. Even in the subjects he recommends for the education of a gentleman, where he was especially following Montaigne, Locke makes a selection, utilitarian in nature and wide in range, that reminds one of the encyclopædic advice of Bacon, Ratich, and Comenius. He

But Locke was also influenced by 'sense realism' to the extent of introducing a utilitarian and encyclopædic curriculum, and in beginning with the vernacular studies and the languages of one's nearest neighbors,

---

[1] Rousseau, however, when he borrowed the suggestion, put it upon the economic ground that if the pupil lost his fortune, he would have the trade to fall back upon.

also resembles the sense realists in desiring to begin with the vernacular studies, which with him are reading, writing, drawing, and possibly shorthand. And when the pupil is able to take up a foreign language, Locke believes, with Comenius, that this should not be Latin, but the language of his nearest neighbor, — in the case of the English boy, French. After the neighboring language has been learned, Latin may be studied. Like the Moravian, too, Locke believes in correlating content studies with the study of languages. He suggests : —

"At the same time that he is learning *French* and *Latin*, a Child, as has been said, may also be enter'd in *Arithmetick, Geography, Chronology, History*, and *Geometry*, too. For if these be taught him in French or Latin, when he begins once to understand either of these tongues, he will get a Knowledge in these sciences, and the Languages to boot."

In the matter of method also, Locke reminds one of Comenius and the other sense realists. He believes that "contrivances might be made *to teach Children to read*, whilst they thought they were only playing," and makes the suggestion of pasting the letters of the alphabet upon the sides of the dice. And further, — "when by these gentle Ways he begins to *read*, some easy pleasant Book, suited to his Capacity, should be put into his Hands, wherein the entertainment he finds might draw him on."

Moreover, Locke is most thoroughly a sense realist in his theory of knowledge and the pedagogical recommenda-

and in his pleasant methods of teaching.

He also holds that impressions are

tions that grow out of it. He holds that impressions are made through the senses by observation, and are only combined afterward by reflection.[1] The development, therefore, of such knowledge to the most complex ideas comes through induction, and in this way the sciences should be studied. In the *Conduct*,[2] he states : —

> "The surest way for a learner, in this as in all other cases, is not to advance by jumps, and large strides; let that which he sets himself to learn next be indeed the next; *i.e.*, as nearly conjoined with what he knows already as it is possible; let it be distinct, but not remote from it; let it be new and what he did not know before, that understanding may advance; but let it be as little at once as may be, that its advances may be clear and sure."

It is not surprising that, with such pleasant methods, Locke, like the realists generally, declares in his *Thoughts* that "great *Severity of Punishment* does but very little Good, nay, great Harm in Education."[3] He prefers "*Esteem* or *Disgrace*" as the proper means of discipline, and maintains, as Comenius did, that corporal punishment should be for moral rather than intellectual remissness.

[margin note: made through the senses by observation.]

[margin note: Discipline should be mild, and not for intellectual remissness.]

[1] This, of course, is brought out more clearly in his philosophical work, *Essay concerning the Human Understanding*.

[2] § XXXIX.

[3] His ideas in the *Conduct* would point to quite a different type of method and discipline.

Locke as the Advocate of ' Formal Discipline '

Locke's real position, however, is found in the mental training of the *Conduct*, and is a reflection of his philosophy, as given in the *Essay*.

Locke, however, cannot be judged to be primarily a realist of either the 'humanistic' or the 'sense' type. His real attitude in education must be taken chiefly from the *Conduct*, and read in the light of his rationalistic philosophy, which, in turn, is directly connected with his view-point in religion and politics. While Locke's ancestry was Puritan, this seems to have had little influence upon his life and philosophy, except as he was ever the advocate of civil, religious, and philosophic freedom. This tendency was increased by his close personal relations with the noted liberal, Lord Shaftesbury. In accordance with his convictions, Locke wrote two *Treatises on Government*, three *Letters on Toleration*, and an essay upon the *Reasonableness of Christianity*. Each of these works vigorously opposed absolutism and dogmatism, but they are all simply applications of the thought underlying his great *Essay concerning the Human Understanding*. In this treatise, which was the product of his reflection during a score of years, he holds, as in the more special works, to the fruitlessness of traditional opinions and empty phraseology. He rejects all 'innate ideas,' or axiomatic principles, and charges that this tenet was imposed by masters and teachers upon their followers, "to take them off their own reason and judgment, and put them on believing and taking them upon trust without further examination." All knowledge, claims the *Essay*, comes rather from experience, and the mind is like "white paper, or wax, to be molded and fashioned as one pleases." [1]   On it ideas are painted by 'sensation' and 'reflection.' Locke further finds it necessary to determine, when the ideas are once in mind, what they tell us in the way of truth. He holds that "knowledge is real only so far as there is a conformity between our ideas and the realities of things," and that, as we cannot always be sure of this correspondence, much of our knowledge is probable and not certain. We must, therefore, in each case carefully consider the grounds of probability, — "the conformity of anything with our own knowledge, observation, and the testimony of others."

To train the mind to make the proper discriminations in these matters, Locke claims that a formal discipline must be furnished by education. This attitude is made clear in his posthumous educational work, *Conduct of the Understanding*. As regards the aim of intellectual education, he holds in his work : —

He holds in his *Conduct* that the mind, like the body, grows through exercise,

"As it is in the body, so it is in the mind; practice makes it what it is, and most even of those excellences which are looked on as natural endowments will be found, when examined into more narrowly, to be the product of exercise, and to be raised to that pitch only by repeated actions. Few men are from their youth

[1] This is his famous doctrine of the *tabula rasa*.

accustomed to strict reasoning, and to trace the dependence of any truth in a long train of consequences to its remote principles and to observe its connection; and he that by frequent practice has not been used to this employment of his understanding, it is no more wonder that he should not, when he is grown into years, be able to bring his mind to it, than that he should not be able on a sudden to grave and design, dance on the ropes, or write a good hand, who has never practiced either of them."

Concerning the best studies for producing this mental gymnastic, Locke says : —

and that the best gymnastics for reasoning is found in mathematics.

"Would you have a man reason well, you must use him to it betimes, exercise his mind in observing the connection of ideas and following them in train. Nothing does this better than mathematics, which therefore I think should be taught all those who have the time and opportunity, not so much to make them mathematicians as to make them reasonable creatures . . ., that having got the way of reasoning, which that study necessarily brings the mind to, they might be able to transfer it to other parts of knowledge as they shall have occasion."

He also advises a range of sciences to dispose the mind so as to be capable of any science.

So Locke advises a wide range of sciences, not for the sake of the realistic knowledge obtained, but for intellectual discipline, "to accustom our minds to all sorts of ideas and the proper ways of examining their habitudes and relations; . . . not to make them perfect in any one of the sciences, but so to open and dispose their minds as may best make them capable of any, when they shall apply themselves to it." Similarly, he implies that reading may become a means of discrimination. "Those who have got this faculty, one may say, have got the true key of books, and the clue to lead them through the mize-maze of variety of opinions and authors to truth and certainty."

The same disciplinary conception of the aim of educa-tion underlies most of Locke's recommendations on moral and physical training in the *Thoughts*. When in this work he comes to treat moral education, he declares at the start: —

Similarly, in the *Thoughts* he declares moral train-ing to be obtained by denying one's desires.

"As the strength of the Body lies chiefly in being able to en-dure Hardships, so also does that of the Mind. And the great Principle and Foundation of all Virtue and Worth is plac'd in this: That a Man is able to *deny* himself his own *Desires*, cross his own Inclinations, and purely follow what Reason directs as Best, tho' the Appetite lean the other Way. . . . This Power is to be got and improv'd by Custom, made easy and familiar by an *early* Practice. If, therefore, I might be heard, I would advise that, contrary to the ordinary Way, Children should be us'd to submit their Desires, and go without their Longings, *even from their very Cradles*. The first Thing they should learn to know, should be that they were not to have any Thing because it pleased them, but because it was thought fit for them."

Hence, in Locke's opinion, morality comes about through submitting the natural desires to the control of reason, and thereby forming virtuous habits. In this light he discusses various virtues and vices as they occur to him, and insists that, in order that the proper habits may be ingrained in them, children should

recognize the absolute authority of their fathers and
tutors.[1]

and physical
training by
the 'harden-
ing process.'

The ideal upon which Locke bases his physical training is even more fully that of formal discipline, and has
since been generally known as the 'hardening process.'
His advice concerning this part of a pupil's training
might be abridged as follows: —

"Most Children's Constitutions are either spoil'd or at least
harm'd by *Cockering* and *Tenderness*.   The first Thing to be taken
Care of is that Children be not *too warmly clad or cover'd*, Winter
or Summer.   The Face when we are born, is no less tender than
any other Part of the Body.   'Tis Use alone hardens it, and
makes it more able to endure the Cold.   I will also advise his
(*i. e.* the child's) *Feet to be wash'd* every Day in cold Water, and
to have his Shoes so thin that they might leak and let in Water,
whenever he comes near it.   I should advise him to play in the
Wind and Sun without a Hat.   His Diet ought to be very plain
and simple, — if he must needs have Flesh, let it be but once a
Day, and of one Sort at a Meal without other Sauce than Hunger.
His Meals should not be kept constantly to an Hour.   Let his
Bed be *hard*, and rather Quilts than feathers, — hard Lodging
strengthens the Parts."

Hence
Locke's real
educational

Thus the intellectual education suggested by Locke
in the *Conduct* is evidently very different in content and

---

[1] Strangely enough, Locke, despite his doctrine of a *tabula rasa*, here
recognizes native tendencies in the child, but they seem to be all hostile
to moral development, and must be 'suppressed,' 'weeded out,' and
'cured.'   Whereas the good elements have in general to be 'imprinted,'
'implanted,' and 'instilled' from the outside.

method from that in his *Thoughts*, by which he is usually measured. And his real educational theory is clearly exhibited in the mental training advocated by the former work and in the positions taken on physical and moral training in the latter. The idea he gives here of training the mind by means of mathematics and other subjects so as to cultivate 'general power,' together with his 'denial of desires' in moral education and the 'hardening process' in physical training, would seem to make Locke the first [1] writer to advocate the doctrine of 'formal discipline.'

The Influence of 'Formal Discipline' upon Education

Adherents of this theory hold that the study of certain subjects yields results out of all proportion to the effort expended, and gives a power that may be applied in any direction. It has been argued by formal disciplinarians, accordingly, that every one should take these all-important studies, regardless of his interest, ability, or purpose in life, and that all who are unfitted for these particular subjects are not qualified for the higher duties and responsibilities, and are unworthy of educational consideration. These subjects are usually held to be the classic languages to improve the 'faculty of memory,' and mathematics to sharpen the 'faculty of reason,'

[1] With possibly the exception of such allusions as appear in Bacon's famous essay, *Of Studies*.

although strenuous efforts have been made by the scientists and others [1] to meet this argument by pointing out the 'formal discipline' in their own favorite studies.

The effect of formal discipline upon the English grammar and public schools, and the universities; the German 'Gymnasien'; and the high schools, colleges, and universities in the United States.

This principle of formal discipline has had a tremendous effect upon each stage of education in practically every country and during every period almost up to the last decade, when a decided reaction began.[2] The formal classicism of the English grammar and public schools and universities, and of the German *Gymnasien*, afford excellent examples of the influence of this doctrine. While in the United States a newer and more flexible society has enabled changes to be more readily made, but a quarter of a century ago Greek, Latin, and mathematics made up most of the course in high schools, colleges, and universities, and until very recently the effete portion of arithmetic and the husks of formal

[1] See *Proceedings of the International Congress of Charities*, 1893, Section VII, where E. B. Andrews makes this argument even for the study of Sociology.

[2] See Adams, *Herbartian Psychology*, Chap. V; Bagley, *Educative Process*, Chaps. XIII–XIV; Heck, *Mental Discipline;* Horne, *Training of the Will* (*School Review*, XIII, pp. 616–628); O'Shea, *Education as Adjustment*, Chaps. XIII and XIV; Thorndike, *Educational Psychology*, Chap. VIII; Wardlow, *Is Mental Discipline a Myth?* (*Educational Review*, XXXV, pp. 22–32). Read also the more recent investigations, which tend to show that we have reacted too far. See the contributions of Angell, Pillsbury, Judd, and Ruediger in *Educational Review*, XXXVI, pp. 1–43, and 364–372, and Winch in the *British Journal of Psychology*, Vol. II, pp. 284–293.

grammar were defended in our elementary education upon the score of 'formal discipline.' But, with the growth of science, the abandonment of the 'faculty' [1] psychology and the development of educational theory, the curriculum has everywhere been broadened, and the content of studies rather than the process of acquisition has come to be emphasized.

It should, however, be recognized that Locke did not defend, but vigorously assailed, the grammatical and linguistic grind in the English public schools. His attitude toward formal discipline sprang from his desire to root out the traditional and false, rather than to support the narrow humanistic curricula of the times. His philosophy and educational doctrines grew out of his purpose to aid the cause of liberty and reason, and his esteem for mathematics as an intellectual training shows his connection with Descartes.[2] It was, moreover, his doctrine that, developed to an extreme, eventuated in the destructive philosophy of the French rationalists and the skepticism of Hume. While, therefore, Locke's imagery of the *tabula rasa* and his disciplinary theory

Yet Locke's formal discipline was not a defense of the public schools, but arose from his desire to root out the traditional and false, and is connected with the rationalism of Descartes and the skepticism of Hume.

[1] See Graves, *History of Education before the Middle Ages*, pp. 196 and 213, for the origin and meaning of the 'faculty' psychology.

[2] Locke had first been stimulated by Descartes, who was reacting from his Jesuit traditions. The effort to strip off preconceived opinions is similar in both, and while Locke rejects the 'innate ideas,' to whose certainty Descartes holds, he also believes in mathematics as the best means of disciplining the mind and of getting rid of the false.

F

have had an influence far beyond his times, it can hardly be supposed that he took that position in conscious support of the conservative formal education of the English schools.   He was in this, as in all his positions, a radical and a rationalist.

SUPPLEMENTARY READING

I. Sources

*Locke, John.   *Some Thoughts concerning Education* (edited by Quick); *Conduct of the Understanding* (edited by Fowler).

II. Authorities

Barnard, H.   *American Journal of Education.*   Vol. V, pp. 209–222.

Browning, O.   *History of Educational Theories.*   Chap. VII.

Compayré, G.   *History of Pedagogy.*   Pp. 194–211.

Davidson, T.   *History of Education.*   Pp. 197–208.

*Fowler, T.   *Locke (English Men of Letters Series).*

Frazer, A. C.   *Locke.*

*Laurie, S. S.   *Educational Opinion since the Renaissance.*   Chaps. XIII–XV.

Munroe, J. P.   *The Educational Ideal.*   Chap. V.

*Quick, R. H.   *Educational Reformers.*   Chap. XIII.

CHAPTER VI

FRANCKE AND HIS INSTITUTIONS

CORRESPONDING to the development of Puritanism in England, a great religious revival also began in Germany toward the close of the seventeenth century. In the midst of the formalism into which Lutheranism had fallen, there arose a set of theologians who were convinced of the need of moral and religious reform, and desired to make religion a matter of life rather than of creed.

Spener and Francke

Among their number early appeared *Philipp Jakob Spener* (1635–1705), a pastor in Frankfurt, who instituted at his home a series of so-called *collegia pietatis* ('religious assemblies'), in which were formulated propositions of reform. The views here represented seem to have been borrowed largely from Puritan writers. They did not advocate any new doctrine, but simply subordinated orthodoxy to spiritual religion and practical morality. The movement spread rapidly, and made a great impression throughout Germany. The old orthodox theologians and pastors were grievously offended, and,

Spener and the rise of Pietism.

from the name of the gatherings, the reformers became known in reproach as *Pietists*.[1]

From the standpoint of education, however, the most important Pietist was *August Hermann Francke* (1663–1727). Francke received an excellent education at the Gotha gymnasium, where he became acquainted with the reforms of Ratich and Comenius, and at the universities of Erfurt, Kiel, and Leipzig, in which he studied theology and the languages, especially Greek and Hebrew. He first came into notice at Leipzig, where he had become a *Privatdocent*,[2] by starting a Pietist society for careful discussion and pious application of the Scriptures. His attitude aroused the ill-will of the older professors and caused his dismissal. After a brief but stormy career as a preacher at Erfurt and as a teacher at Hamburg, he assisted in founding the University of Halle, which became the center from which Pietism was diffused throughout Germany.

Organization of Francke's Institutions

Here in 1692 Francke became a professor of the Greek and Hebrew languages, but was afterward transferred to his favorite subject of theology. To make ends meet,

[1] Like the names *Puritan* and *Methodist*, however, it was afterward adopted as a term of honor.

[2] In the German universities a *Privatdocent* is not, like a professor, in receipt of a regular salary, but is given a percentage of the fees of the students that attend his lectures.

he was also appointed pastor in the suburb of Glaucha, *'Armenschule,' a*
and through this latter position his real work as an edu- *'Bürgerschule,' and a*
cator began. While catechizing the children who came *'Waisenanstalt.'*
to the parsonage to beg, he was shocked at their ignorance,
poverty, and immorality, and resolved to raise them
from their degradation by education. One day early in
1695, upon finding a contribution of seven guldens[1]
in his alms box, he started an *Armenschule* ('school
for the poor') in his own house, and engaged a student
of the university as its teacher. As he was soon requested to open another school for those whose parents
could afford to pay, he rented two rooms in a neighboring building, — one for the *Armenschule* and one for
the *Bürgerschule* ('school for citizens'). Further, believing it of advantage to remove orphans from their old
associations, he established a third institution for them,
called the *Waisenanstalt* ('orphanage'), and later he sub-
divided all three organizations upon the basis of sex.

Still in this same year, he undertook for a wealthy *He also
founded*
widow of noble family to educate her son together with *secondary
schools, —*
some other boys, and his work in this direction grew *'Pädago-*

---

[1] The silver *Gulden*, or ' florin,' worth about forty cents, would seem to
be meant here. $2.80 seems a small sum with which to ' found a school,'
but in Francke's time a coin of the present value of a dollar had a very
large purchasing power. With the contribution, we learn, Francke purchased two thalers' (about $1.50) worth of books and employed a poor
student to teach the children two hours daily. For the further support
of the school he declared he would ' trust God.'

gium,'
'Schola
Latina,'
'Töchter-
schule,' and
'Realschule,'

rapidly into a secondary school, which came to be known as the *Pädagogium*. Two years later he started another secondary course for the purpose of preparing the brighter boys from the orphan and poor schools for the university, and this was called the *Lateinische Hauptschule*, or *Schola Latina*, to distinguish it from the elementary schools, in which no foreign language was taught. As early as 1698, Francke likewise wished to organize a boarding-school where girls whose parents could afford it might obtain a training in Latin, Greek, Hebrew, and other secondary subjects, and while at first this enterprise was on a small scale, within a dozen years the *Höhere Töchterschule* ('higher school for girls') became a regular part of his system. Moreover, through his colleague, Semler, a secondary school of a more practical type, called the *Realschule*, in which the pure and applied sciences were taught, became associated in 1708 with the institutions of Francke.

In addition to these elementary and secondary schools, Francke was also enabled, through a gift of four thousand marks ($1000), to institute in 1695 a *Seminarium Præceptorum* ('seminary for teachers'), in which the theological students that taught in his schools might be trained. These students practiced teaching for two hours each day under the supervision and criticism of inspectors, and were boarded at a *Freitisch* ('free table'), established by means of the endowment.

and a 'Semi-
narium Præ-
ceptorum.'

His Religious Aim in Education

Even if we were not acquainted with the origin of Pietism, or with the practice in Francke's schools, the explicit statements in his *Brief and Simple Treatise on Christian Education* [1] would make it evident that the educational aim underlying all his work was primarily religious training. "The chief object in view," says Francke, "is that all children may be instructed above all things in the vital knowledge of God and Christ, and be initiated into the principles of true religion." He goes so far as to insist : —

His *Christian Education* holds religion to be the chief aim, but declares that the pupil's station must be considered.

"Only the pious man is a good member of society. Without sincere piety, all knowledge, all prudence, all worldly culture, is more hurtful than useful, and we are never secure against its misuse."

His position is, therefore, a real return to the Reformation emphasis upon faith and non-ceremonial worship. Nevertheless, it has been clear that he was sufficiently affected by the times to found his schools somewhat with reference to existing social strata, and he distinctly declares, "In all instruction we must keep the pupil's station and future calling in mind."

Course and Methods in His Schools

Naturally, then, the subject most emphasized in all of Francke's schools was religion. In the elementary

The Bible and catechism as material, and

[1] The full title is *Kurzer und einfältiger Unterricht wie die Kinder zur wahren Gottseligkeit und Christlichen Klugheit anzuführen sind.*

reading and writing based on the Scriptures.

schools, four out of seven hours each day were given to Bible study, catechism, prayer, and pious observances, and the reading and writing were based upon the Scriptures as material. After learning to read, a pupil studied arithmetic for four hours, and vocal music for two hours each week. Incidentally, the course was enriched with

Realistic studies.

a knowledge of 'real' or useful things, such as the simplest facts of astronomy and physics, bits of geographical and historical information, and various household arts.

In the ' Pädagogium,' Greek and Hebrew for exegesis, and Latin and French through the Bible.

In the *Pädagogium*, not only was religion the chief study, but Greek and Hebrew were taught largely for the sake of exegesis, compositions were written in Latin upon Bible subjects, and French was learned through a New Testament in that language. The realistic turn to Francke's work also appeared in training in the vernacular, in such studies as mathematics, German oratory, history, and geography, and in the elements of natural science, arts, and crafts, and of astronomy, anatomy,

Realistic and practical studies.

and materia medica. He also added the management of estates, gardens, and vineyards, and such other knowledge as the upper classes of society would find useful. As the pupils in the *Schola Latina* were not of sufficient social standing to demand it, the French and some of the practical studies of the *Pädagogium* were omitted,

Course of the ' Schola Latina,' the ' Realschule,' and the

but the curriculum was otherwise the same. The *Realschule* went more fully into the mathematics, sciences, and useful subjects than did the *Pädagogium*. The work in the *Töchterschule* was not unlike that in the Latin school, but included the household arts and other occupational studies and 'accomplishments.'

While the course in all of Francke's schools was distinctly disciplinary in theory, good pedagogy was not altogether neglected. The teachers were directed by his treatise to study each individual pupil, and were advised how to train children to concentrate, observe, and reason. Although much memorizing was practiced, "children were not to be permitted to learn to prattle words without understanding them." This comprehension of the work was, of course, increased by applying all studies to everyday life. The pupils wrote formal letters, receipts, and bonds, and their mathematical problems were based upon practical transactions. The discipline in all the schools of Francke, in consequence, though strict, was mild and humane.

The Influence of Francke's Institutions

From these schools, together with the orphanage, seminary, and 'free table' as a nucleus, have developed the now celebrated organization known as *Franckesche Stiftungen* ('Francke's Institutions'). "It is difficult to decide," says Adamson, "whether the most surprising feature is their humble beginning, or their rapid growth and steady adaptation of means to ends." In spite of many controversies resulting from the Pietistic auspices of the institutions, at the death of Francke in 1727 there were already in the elementary schools some seventeen hundred and twenty-five pupils of both sexes, in the orphanage were maintained one hundred boys and thirty-four girls, while the *Pädagogium* had eighty-two, and the *Schola Latina* four hundred boys, and two hundred and fifty students boarded at the 'free table.'

These institutions have since been increased in number, and there are now some twenty-five enterprises conducted in a large group of structures built about a double court. Among the additions are a printing plant and bindery, a bookstore, a Bible house, a drug store and dispensary, and a home for women, as well as a *Realgymnasium*[1] and a *Vorschule*.[2] Through these institutions more than four thousand persons are being provided with the means of an education or livelihood, and many good causes are advanced. Over one million marks ($250,000), coming from the endowment, state appropriations, tuition fees, and profits upon the enterprises, are expended each year in maintaining the institutions.

The 'modern' studies have influ-

This work of Francke has had a great influence upon German education in several directions. The 'modern'

---

[1] A compromise between the *Gymnasium* and the *Realschule*, which has been quite common in Germany, but is now disappearing.

[2] A preparatory school for the secondary schools, attended by children between six and nine.

studies of the *Pädagogium* and *Schola Latina* have been a model for Prussia and all Protestant Germany, and have somewhat affected the curricula of the *Gymnasien*. The *Realschule* of Semler was brought in a slightly modified form to Berlin by Hecker, one of the teachers in the *Pädagogium*. From the capital it spread gradually throughout Prussia, until it was taken into the public system, and is to-day one of the most important features. The seminary, or training school for teachers, has been adopted by practically every one of the German states. Further, since in the various schools of Francke were realized the chief ideals of most educational reformers up to that time, Germany was thereby given a concrete example of what it might best strive to imitate. Again, by means of teachers trained in his system at the seminary, all Germany has been leavened with the spirit of the great Pietist.

As to Pietism itself, however, while originally a protest against creed and ceremonial, in later years it lost much of its living power and deteriorated into a formalism in religious life and thought. It magnified even the smallest of daily doings into expressions of piety, and became, like Puritanism, pervaded with affectation and cant. To a great extent its schools, with their spiritual purpose and content, then lapsed into merely inefficient classes in formal catechism, and all hold upon real living was lost. The religious revival of Spener and the edu-

[margin notes] enced the 'Gymnasien'; the 'Realschule' has spread throughout Prussia; and the 'Seminarium' has been adopted by practically all the German states.

All Germany has been leavened.

But Pietism itself became crystallized and fixed.

cational impulse of Francke had become crystallized and fixed.

SUPPLEMENTARY READING

I. SOURCES

KRAMER, G. (Editor).   *A. H. Francke's Pädagogische Schriften.*

RICHTER, A.   *August Hermann Francke, Kurzer und Einfältiger Unterricht* (Pt. X of *Neudrücke Pädagogischer Schriften*).

II. AUTHORITIES

*ADAMSON, J. W.   *Pioneers of Modern Education.*   Chap. XIII.

COMPAYRÉ, G.   *History of Pedagogy.*   P. 414.

FRANCKE, K.   *German Literature as Determined by Social Forces.* Pp. 175-176.

KRAMER, G.   *August Hermann Francke; ein Lebensbild* and *Francke und seine Stiftungen in Halle* (*A. H. Francke's Pädagogische Schriften*, Introduction).

NOHLE, E.   *History of the German School System.*   (*Report of the United States Commissioner of Education.*   1897-1898, pp. 49-51).

*QUICK, R. H.   *Educational Reformers.*   Chap. XIII.

RUSSELL, J. E.   *German Higher Schools.*   Pp. 63-65.

WILLIAMS, S. G.   *History of Modern Education.*   Pp. 259-272.

CHAPTER VII

ROUSSEAU AND NATURALISM IN EDUCATION

THE inconsistencies and contradictions of Rousseau are almost proverbial. But in his antecedents and career can be found a ready explanation for the positions of this most illogical writer. The theories of no man are more clearly a product of his heredity, experience, and times, and, thanks to his own mercilessly frank *Confessions*,[1] there are few instances in history where the life and environment of any other personage are known in so much detail.

The Life, Training, and Times of Rousseau

Jean Jacques Rousseau (1712–1778) was born of upper-class parentage in the simple Protestant city of Geneva. His father, a watchmaker, was descended from a Parisian family, and inherited much of the romanticism, mercurial temperament, and love of pleasure of his forbears. The mother of Rousseau, too, although the daughter of a clergyman, was of a morbid and sentimental disposition.

The parentage and training of Rousseau tended to make him emotional, imaginative, and precocious.

---

[1] The *Confessions* carry his life from early childhood up to his expulsion from the Ile de Saint Pierre and his preparation to go to Hume. See p. 104. We are largely dependent upon the *Reveries* and *Letters* for the rest of his biography.

77

She died at the birth of Jean Jacques, and the child was brought up by an indulgent aunt, who made little attempt to correct his pilfering and lying, and utterly failed to instil in him any real moral principles. This general tendency toward a want of self-control was further increased by the careless attitude of his father. While the boy was but six, the elder Rousseau sat up with him night after night until daylight reading the silliest and most sensational of romances from the extensive collection left by his wife. Thus were nurtured within the child an extreme emotionality, imaginativeness, and precocity. After a year or so the novels were exhausted, and Rousseau was forced to turn for material to the more sensible library of his grandfather, the preacher. The works the child found here, such as the *Parallel Lives* of Plutarch and the standard histories of the day, made quite as profound an impression upon his character. They contributed to his sense of heroism and what he afterward termed "that republican spirit and love of liberty, that haughty and invincible turn of mind, which rendered me impatient of restraint." His want of control may in this way have first come to turn itself toward revolution and the destruction of existing society.

His environment cultivated a love of nature, and the theory that

The two years following this period Jean Jacques spent in the village of Bossey, just outside Geneva, where he had been sent with a cousin of about the same age to be educated. Here his love of nature, which had already been cultivated by the beauties of Genevan environment, was greatly heightened. He found a wonderful enjoyment in this rural life, until a severe punishment for a boyish offense turned all to dross. Thereupon, he declares, he began to evolve the theory that it is through restraint and discipline of the impulses and departure from nature that humanity has ever been corrupted and ruined, and it may well be that later on, from his adult standpoint, this experience seemed to have contributed to what then became the central feature of his philosophy.

departure from nature had corrupted humanity.

After this the boy returned to Geneva and spent a couple of years in idleness and sentimentality. Then, during trade apprenticeships lasting four years, he was further corrupted by low companions and gave free rein to his impulses to loaf, lie, and steal. Eventually, he ran away from the city, and spent several years in vagrancy, dissoluteness, and menial service. During this time the beauties of nature were more than ever impressed upon the youth by the wonderful scenery of the Savoy country through which he passed, and his education was somewhat improved by incidental instruction from a relative of one of the families he served. Finally, at nineteen, Rousseau went to stay in Savoy with Madame de Warens, a person of shallow character and considerable beauty. In the decade he lived there, under most anomalous conditions, upon the meager pension of a woman, he obtained further sporadic train-

His want of self-control, love of nature, and sympathy with the oppressed, were strengthened by his wanderings.

ing in Latin, music, philosophy, and some of the sciences.
Through occasional wanderings he also strengthened
his love of nature and learned to sympathize with the
condition of the poor and oppressed. At length he and
Madame de Warens grew tired of each other, and Rousseau gravitated to Paris. In this city he was forced to
earn a livelihood for himself and Thérèse Le Vasseur, a
coarse and stupid servant girl, with whom he lived for
the rest of his life. He thus began to develop some sense
of responsibility.

His attitude
blended well
with the
vague senti-
ments of the
period.

While Rousseau's days of vagabondage were now over,
they had left an ineffaceable stamp upon him. His
sensitiveness, impulsiveness, love for nature, and sympathy for the poor, together with his inaccurate and unsystematic education, were ever afterward in evidence.
And it can be seen that these characteristics of Rousseau blended well with a body of inchoate sentiments
and vague longings of this period that were striving for
expression. These were the days of Louis XV and royal
absolutism, when the administration of all affairs in the
kingdom was controlled nominally by the monarch, but
really by a small clique of idle and extravagant courtiers
about him. It was necessary for those who had any
desire for advancement to seek to attach themselves to
the court and adopt its elaborate rules and customs. In
consequence, a most artificial system of etiquette and
conduct had grown up everywhere in the upper class of

society. Under this veneer and extreme conventionality were the degraded peasants, ground down by taxation, deprived of their rights, and obliged to minister to the pleasure of a vicious leisure class. But against this oppression and decadence there had gradually arisen an undefined spirit of protest and a tendency to hark back to simpler conditions. There had come into the air a feeling that the despotism and artificiality of the times were due to the departure of civilized man from an original beneficent state of nature, and that above all legislation and institutions was a natural law in complete harmony with the divine will. Hence it happened that Rousseau, emotional, uncontrolled, and half-trained, was destined to bring to consciousness and give voice to the revolutionary and naturalistic ideas and tendencies of the century.

His Discourses, and *The New Heloise, Social Contract,* and *Emile*

For some time, among other methods of securing a living, he had been attempting literary production, when by a curious accident in 1750 he leaped into fame as a writer. The preceding year the Academy of Dijon[1] had proposed as a theme for a prize essay : *Has the progress of the sciences and arts contributed to corrupt or to*

Finally at Paris his chaotic thought was crystallized in his essay on The Progress of the Sciences and Arts in

[1] A few of the larger cities of France had, in imitation of Paris, founded 'academies' for the discussion of scientific and philosophic questions. Of these institutions one of the earliest and most prominent was that of Dijon.

G

1750 and his
essay on
Inequality
three years
later.

purify morals? [1]   This inquiry seems to have suddenly
brought to a focus all the chaotic thought that had been
surging within Rousseau, and with much fervor and con-
viction, though most illogically, he declared that the
existing oppression and corruption of society were due
to the advancement of civilization.   In the discourse
written by him he contrasts the rugged conduct of men
in the primitive ages with the artificial manners of his
day, under which were cloaked impiety, deception, and
arrogance.   He undertakes to show from the history of
the Oriental and classical nations that this degeneracy
has ever been caused by the development of the arts and
sciences and the attempt to pass from that happy state
of ignorance in which men are placed by nature.   Rousseau's essay won the prize and created a tremendous
stir.   Three years later he competed for another prize
offered by the same academy on the subject: *The origin
of inequality among men.* [2]   In his discourse on this subject
Rousseau holds that the physical and intellectual in-
equalities of nature which existed in primitive society were
scarcely noticeable, but that, with the growth of civilization, most oppressive distinctions arose, especially through
the institution of private property.   He declares: —

"The first man who, having inclosed a piece of ground, could
think of saying, 'This is mine,' and found people simple enough to

[1] *Si le progrès des sciences et des arts a contribué à corrompre ou à épurer
les mœurs.*   [2] *L'origine de l'inégalité parmi les hommes.*

believe him, was the real founder of civil society. How many crimes, wars, murders, miseries, and horrors would not have been spared to the human race by any one who, pulling up the stakes or filling in the trench, could have called out to his fellows: 'Beware of listening to this impostor; you are undone if you forget that the earth belongs to no one, and that its fruits are for all!'"

For, he claims, it is the institution of property that soon led to robbery and insecurity, and this brought about civilization and laws to protect the accumulations of the wealthy. Through a law-governed society the poor were thrown more deeply into bondage and a new power was added to the rich.[1]

As Rousseau's democratic and revolutionary spirit developed, Paris, with its hypocritical and cold-blooded atmosphere, became more and more stifling to him. Finally, in 1756, he withdrew to the village of Montmorency and the society of devoted friends. Here in 1761, after a period of idleness and a most unfortunate

After withdrawing to Montmorency, he produced by 1762 The New Heloise, Social Contract, and Emile, which

---

[1] The following ironical letter written by Voltaire to Rousseau concerning this work exposes the fundamental weakness of the author's philosophy :—

"I have received your new book against the human race and thank you for it. Never was such cleverness used in the design of making us all stupid. One longs on reading your book to walk on all fours. But as I have lost that habit for more than sixty years, I feel unhappily the impossibility of renewing it. Nor can I embark in search of the savages of Canada, because the maladies to which I am condemned render a European surgeon necessary to me; because war is going on in those regions; and because the example of our actions has made the savages nearly as bad as ourselves."

modify some-
what his idea
of a complete
return to
nature. love affair, he produced his remarkable romance, *The New Heloise*,[1] and in the following year his influential essay on political ethics, known as the *Social Contract*,[2] and that most revolutionary treatise on education, the *Emile*. *The New Heloise* departs somewhat from the complete return to nature sought in the two discourses. It commends a restoration of as much of the primitive simplicity of living as the crystallized traditions and institutions of society will permit. While the first part of the work is filled with passion and illicit love,[3] the last is an exaltation of marriage and the family, and of the happiness and peace of rural life. In the *Social Contract*, Rousseau also finds the ideal state, not in that of nature, but in a society managed by the people, where simplicity and natural wants control, and aristocracy and artificiality do not exist. A state of nature, however, is still the starting-point. Civilized society originated when men in the primitive condition found the obstacles to self-preservation too strong, and sought by association to protect the person and property of all. The body thus constituted is sovereign, and every citizen is a member of it. The government which it sets up, whether a monarchy, aristocracy, or democracy, may, therefore, be abolished at any time by the general will

---

[1] The full title was *Julie, ou la nouvelle Héloise*.   [2] *Contrât Social*.

[3] The second part of the title grows out of this resemblance to the story of Abelard and Heloise.

of the people. The furore that this doctrine created in church and monarch-ridden France can easily be imagined.

The Purpose of the *Emile*

But the work that has made the name of Rousseau famous and most concerns us here is his *Emile*. This treatise and the two discourses their author declared to be "three inseparable works, which together form a single whole." He might well have included also the *New Heloise* and the *Social Contract*, especially as the *Emile* assumes more nearly the modified position of the later works, and undertakes to show how education might minimize the drawbacks of civilization and bring man as near to nature as possible. As the *Social Contract* and his discourses were written to counteract the oppressive social and political conditions, the *Emile* aims to replace the conventional and formal education of the day with a training that should be natural and spontaneous. We learn that under this *ancien régime* little boys had their hair powdered, wore a sword, ' the chapeau under the arm, a frill, and a coat with gilded cuffs,' that a girl was dressed in equally ridiculous imitation of a fashionable woman, and that education was largely one of deportment and the dancing master, for "this is to be the great thing for them when they become men and women, and for this reason it is the thing of chief impor-

The Emile was directed against the artificial education of the day, and applies Rousseau's naturalism to education.

tance for them as children." [1] On the intellectual side, education was largely traditional and consisted chiefly of a training in Latin grammar, words, and *memoriter* work. Rousseau scathingly criticized these practices and pleaded for reform. Hence in the *Emile* he applies his naturalistic principles to the education of an imaginary pupil of that name "from the moment of his birth up to the time when, having become a mature man, he will no *It is divided into five parts:* longer need any other guide than himself." The work is divided into five parts, four of which deal with Emile's education in the stages of infancy, childhood, boyhood, and youth respectively, and the fifth with the training of the girl who is to become his wife.

The Five Books of the *Emile*

(1) 'infancy,' when the pupil is to be removed from society, and given a natural and physical training; Rousseau starts the first book with a re-statement of his basal principle that "everything is good as it comes from the hands of the Author of Nature; but everything degenerates in the hands of man." After elaborating this, he shows that we are educated by "three kinds of teachers, — nature, men, and things, and since the co-operation of the three educations is necessary for their perfection, it is to the one over which we have no control (*i.e.* nature) that we must direct the other two."

[1] Taine, *The Ancient Régime*, p. 137. Read S. C. Parker's clear presentation of this 'dancing-master education' in *The Elementary School Teacher*, Vol. X, pp. 139–148.

Education must, therefore, conform to nature, and must be a means not of preparing for citizenship in any particular government, much less for an occupation, but of developing manhood and fitting for 'the duties of human life.' "To live," says Rousseau of his pupil, "is the trade I wish to teach him." For so delicate a task the training of the child must be undertaken by his parents, or if, as in the case of Emile, he is an orphan, by a trustworthy tutor, who can secure his full confidence.[1] As an infant, Emile must be removed to the country, where he will be close to nature and farthest from the contaminating influences of civilization. His growth and training must be as spontaneous as possible. He must have nothing to do with either medicine or doctors, "unless his life is in evident danger; for then they can do nothing worse than kill him." His natural movements must not be restrained by caps, bands, or swaddling clothes, and he should be nursed by his own mother.[2]

[1] It is clear from the mention of a tutor that Rousseau had in mind reforming only the unnatural education of the upper class. With all his sympathy for the downtrodden peasants, he did not feel the need of improving their training. He is rather impressed with their opportunity for free development, saying, "The poor man needs no education, for his condition forces one upon him."

[2] The effect of this teaching of Rousseau upon the fashionable French mothers was not altogether happy. When this 'return to nature' came to be a fad, these ladies did not abandon society, but had the infants brought in at dessert, when the mothers were filled with wine and food, or in the intervals of the dance, when they were overheated, and gave

He should likewise be used to baths of all sorts of temperature.   In fact, the child should not be forced into any fixed ways whatsoever, since, with Rousseau, habit is necessarily something contrary to impulse and so unnatural and a thing to be shunned.   "The only habit," says he, "which the child should be allowed to form is to contract no habit whatsoever."   Since, however, ugly objects, alarming sounds, and the dark exist in nature, he should be gradually accustomed to them.   When he cries for a reason, he should be cared for, but when from caprice or obstinacy, he should not be heeded, or, if it is necessary to divert his attention, it should be without his suspecting it.   His playthings should not be "gold or silver bells, coral, elaborate crystals, toys of all kinds and prices," but such simple products of nature as "branches with their fruits and flowers, or a poppy-head in which the seeds are heard to rattle."   Language that is simple, plain, and hence natural, should be used with him, and he should not be hurried beyond nature in learning to talk.   He should be restricted to a few words that express real thoughts for him.

The education of Emile during infancy is thus to be purely physical.   The aim is simply to keep his instincts

them their natural sustenance at that time.   Nevertheless, Rousseau did permanently modify the attitude toward children and the treatment of them.   Parents entered into more intimate relations with their children and found time to look after their education.

and impulses, which, Rousseau holds, are good by nature, free from vice, and his intelligence free from error. This natural and negative education is continued in the second book, which deals with the child between the years of five and twelve. No moral training is to be given as such, for "until he reaches the age of reason, he can form no idea of moral beings or social relations." Rousseau maintains that "the terms obey and command are proscribed from his vocabulary, and still more the terms duty and obligation." Certain lessons are, however, to be taught him indirectly by a control of his environment, for "the terms force, necessity, impotency, and constraint should have a large place" with him, and "he is to be taught by experience." He is to learn through 'natural consequences' until he arrives at the age for understanding moral precepts. If he breaks the furniture or the windows, let him suffer the inconveniences that arise from his act. Do not preach to him or punish him for lying, but afterward affect not to believe him even when he has spoken the truth. If he carelessly digs up the sprouting melons of the gardener, in order to plant beans for himself, let the gardener in turn uproot the beans, and thus cause him to learn the sacredness of property. In intellectual matters, too, Rousseau condemns the usual unnatural practice of requiring pupils to learn so much before they have reached the proper years. He rhetorically asks: "Shall I venture to state at this point

(2) 'childhood,' between five and twelve, when he is to be given no moral training, but to learn through 'consequences,' and to develop the body rather than the mind;

the most important, the most useful, rule of all education? It is not to gain time, but to lose it." Hence during this period Emile is not to study geography, history, or languages, upon which pedagogues ordinarily depend to exhibit the attainments of their pupils, although these understand nothing of what they have memorized. He is not to commit fables to memory, for he will be very likely to misapply the moral. Rousseau even goes so far as to declare : —

"In thus relieving children of all their school tasks, I take away the instrument of their greatest misery, namely, books. Reading is the scourge of childhood, and almost the sole occupation that we know how to give them. At the age of twelve, Emile will hardly know what a book is. But I shall be told that it is very necessary that he know how to read. This I grant. It is necessary that he know how to read when reading is useful to him. Until then, it serves only to annoy him."

The chief function of education at this period is to develop the body and "keep the soul fallow," for, "in order to think, we must exercise our limbs, our senses, and our organs, which are the instruments of our intelligence." To obtain this training, Emile is to wear short, loose, and scanty clothing, go bareheaded, and have the body inured to cold and heat, and be generally subjected to a 'hardening process' similar to that recommended by Locke.[1] He should have plenty of time for sleep, although he should learn to have it interrupted and to

[1] See p. 62.

endure a hard bed. He must learn to swim, to protect himself from drowning, and must prepare for emergencies, by practicing long and high jumps, leaping walls, and scaling rocks. His senses are to be exercised on natural problems in weighing and measuring masses and distances; his hand and eye are to be trained by drawing from nature about him, and his ear is to be rendered sensitive to harmony by learning to sing.

There comes, however, between twelve and fifteen, after the boy's body and senses have been trained, "an interval when the power of the individual is greater than his desires, which is the period of his greatest relative strength." This period, which is dealt with in his third book, Rousseau declares, is intended by nature itself as "the time of labor, instruction, and study." But it is obvious even to our unpractical author that not much can be learned within three years, and he accordingly decides to limit instruction to "merely that which is useful." And even of useful studies the boy should not be expected to learn those "truths which require, for being comprehended, an understanding already formed, or which dispose an inexperienced mind to think falsely on other subjects." After eliminating all useless, incomprehensible, and misleading studies, Rousseau finds that natural sciences alone remain as `mental pabulum for the boy. The natural method for acquiring these subjects, he believes, is through an

(3) ' boyhood,' between twelve and fifteen, when he is to learn only useful studies without books of any sort, save *Robinson Crusoe,* and to take up the trade of cabinetmaking.

appeal to the curiosity and instinct for investigation.
"Ask questions that are within his comprehension, and
leave him to resolve them. Let him know nothing
because you have told it to him, but because he has
comprehended it himself; he is not to learn science,
but to discover it. If you ever substitute in his mind
authority for reason, he will no longer reason." So
Rousseau contrasts the current methods of teaching
astronomy and geography by means of globes, maps,
and other misleading representations, with the more
natural plan of stimulating inquiry by observing the
sun when rising and setting during the different seasons,
and by studying the topography of the neighborhood
and drawing maps of it. Emile is taught to appreciate
the value of these subjects by being lost in the forest,
and, in his efforts to find a way out, discovering a use
for them. He learns the elements of electricity by
meeting with a juggler, who attracts an artificial duck
by means of a concealed magnet. He similarly dis-
covers through experience the effect of cold and heat
upon solids and liquids, and so comes to understand the
thermometer and other instruments. Hence Rousseau
feels that all knowledge of real value may be acquired
clearly and naturally without the use of rivalry or textbooks. "I hate books," he says; "they merely teach
us to talk of what we do not know." But he finds one
book, "where all the natural needs of man are exhibited

in a manner obvious to the mind of a child, and where the means of providing for these needs are successively developed with the same facility." This book, *Robinson Crusoe*,[1] should be carefully studied by Emile. In order to learn the interdependence of men from the industrial rather than the moral side, Emile and his tutor now also labor in the various arts, and that he may be independent of changes in fortune and revolutions in government, the boy is to learn a trade. Cabinet-making, as being 'nearest to the state of nature' and most capable of exercising both mind and body, is chosen.

Emile is now fifteen, and his mind is prepared to receive an ethical training. This is treated in the fourth book, which is the most brilliant and chimerical of all. The motive of education has hitherto been self-interest, and the object self-development. Emile must now learn to live with others and be trained in social relationships. He is to be made affectionate, moral, and religious. "We have formed his body, his senses, and his intelligence; it remains to give him a heart." The supreme importance of the adolescent period for this moral training is recognized by Rousseau in the declaration : —

(4) 'youth,' from fifteen on, when he is to be made moral and religious, by visits to unfortunates, exposure to knaves, the use of fables, and the adoption of deism;

"This critical time, though very short, has lasting influences. Here is the second birth of which I have spoken; it is here that

[1] Thus Campe of the 'Philanthropinum,' which attempted to put Rousseau's doctrines into practice, wrote on the model of *Robinson Crusoe* the work now known as *Swiss Family Robinson*. See p. 115.

man really begins to live, and nothing human is foreign to him. So far our cares have been but child's play; it is only now that they assume a real importance. This epoch, where ordinary education ends, is properly one where ours ought to begin."

"To turn his character toward benevolence and goodness" during this impressionable age, Rousseau declares, is to be accomplished not through precepts, but in a natural way by bringing the youth into contact with his fellow men and appealing to his emotions. Emile is to visit infirmaries, hospitals, and prisons, and witness concrete examples of wretchedness in all stages, although not so frequently as to become hardened. That this training may not render him cynical or hypercritical, it should be corrected by the study of history, where one sees men simply as a spectator without feeling or passion. Further, in order to deliver Emile from vanity, so common during adolescence, he is to be exposed to flatterers, spendthrifts, and sharpers, and allowed to suffer the consequences. He may at this time also be guided in his conduct by the use of fables, for "by censuring the wrongdoer under an unknown mask, we instruct without offending him." In a similarly indirect and informal fashion Emile is to be given his religious education. Until now he has been taught nothing about God or the human soul, as Rousseau holds that "it would be much better to have no idea of the Divinity than to have ideas which are low, fanciful, wrongful, or unworthy of him." But now "the natural progress of his intelligence carries his researches in that direction" and "from the study of nature he comes without difficulty to a search for its Author." Under the guise of the *Savoyard Vicar's* [1] *Profession of Faith* Rousseau describes the deism, or naturalistic views, which his pupil is to adopt. This formulation, which is written in stately but impassioned language, while departing from the position of the traditionalized Church of the day, is not, like the attacks of the rationalists, merely destructive. It seeks to replace organized Christianity with a natural and undogmatic religion. The vicar declares : —

"I perceive God everywhere in his works; I feel him in myself; I see him universally around me. But when I fain would seek where he is, what he is, of what substance, he glides away from me, and my troubled soul discerns nothing. The less I can conceive him, the more I adore. I bow myself down, and say to him, O being of beings, I am because thou art; to meditate ceaselessly on thee by day and by night is to raise myself to my veritable source and fount."

Emile at length becomes a man, and a life companion must be found for him. A search should be made for a

and (5), the education of woman, since

---

[1] This vicar of Savoy was a kindly old priest, who undertook to counsel Rousseau when at the height of his reckless career in Turin. Rousseau was much impressed, and afterward put his highest conception of religion into the mouth of this spiritual adviser. It fills a large portion of the fourth book.

now that Emile has become a man, a life companion who has been suitably trained must be found for him.

suitable lady, but "in order to find her, we must know her." Accordingly, the last book of the *Emile* deals with the model Sophie and the education of woman. It is the weakest part of his work, for here Rousseau completely abandons the individualistic training to be given the man. He insists:—

"The whole education of women ought to be relative to men. To please them, to be useful to them, to make themselves loved and honored by them, to educate them when young, to care for them when grown, to counsel them, to console them, to make life agreeable and sweet to them — these are the duties of women at all times, and what should be taught them from infancy."

Like men, women should be given adequate bodily training, but rather for the sake of physical charms and of producing vigorous offspring than for their own development. Their instinctive love of pleasing through dress should be made of service by teaching them sewing, embroidery, lace-work, and designing. Further, "girls ought to be obedient and industrious, and they ought early to be brought under restraint. Made to obey a being so imperfect as man, often so full of vices, and always so full of faults, they ought early to learn to suffer even injustice, and endure the wrongs of a husband without complaint." Girls should be taught singing, dancing, and other accomplishments that will make them attractive without interfering with their submissiveness. They should be instructed dogmatically in religion at an early age. "Every daughter should have the religion of her mother, and every wife that of her husband." In ethical matters they should be largely guided by public opinion. A woman may not learn philosophy, art, or science, but she should study men. "She must learn to penetrate their feelings through their conversation, their actions, their looks, and their gestures, and know how to give them the feelings which are pleasing to her, without even seeming to think of them."

Such was Rousseau's notion of a natural and individualistic education for a man and the passive and repressive training suitable for a woman, and of the happiness and prosperity that were bound to ensue.[1] To make a fair estimate of the *Emile* is not easy. It is necessary to put aside all of one's prejudices against the weak and offensive personality of the author and to view the contradictions of his life and writings in their true perspective. His work on education is probably the most extraordinary union of strength and weakness, fascination and repulsion, high ideals and unpracticality,

The defects in the Emile are outweighed by its merits:

---

[1] Later on, Rousseau seems to have had misgivings as to the effect of this training, and started a work called *Emile and Sophie, or the Solitaries*. This consists of a series of letters from Emile to his tutor, in which Rousseau endeavors to show how, even if adversity should overtake his pupil, the natural education would still be the best. At every turn Emile rises superior to his misfortunes, exhibits the most valuable knowledge and resources, and comes rapidly into places of honor and emolument.

H

that was ever produced.   But its errors and illusions are fully outweighed by great truths and lofty sentiments, and, in making an appraisal, one should offset the grave defects of the book by its still larger merits.

The Merits and Defects of the *Emile*

It is most
illogical, but
brilliant and
convincing.

The *Emile*, it must be admitted at the start, is often illogical, erratic, and inconsistent.   Rousseau constantly sways from optimism to pessimism, from spontaneity to authority, from liberalism to intolerance.   While he holds that society is thoroughly corrupt, he has great confidence in the goodness of all individuals of which it is composed. In the face of history and psychology, he opposes nature to culture, and creates a dualism between emotion and reason.   Although the instincts and re-actions of Emile are apparently given free play, they are really under the constant guidance of his tutor. The supposed isolation of the pupil is conveniently for-gotten on occasion by attendance at fairs, parties, and competitions with his fellows.   Emile is to have his individuality developed to its utmost, but Sophie's is to be trained out of her.   However, in spite of such glaring inconsistencies, the *Emile* has at all times been ac-counted a work of great richness and power.   The brilliant thought, the underlying wisdom of many of his suggestions, the sentimental appeal, and the clear, enthusiastic, and ardent presentation have completely overbalanced its contradictions and logical deficiencies.

The most marked feature of the Rousselian education and the one most subject to criticism has been its extreme revolt against civilization and all social control. A state of nature is held to be the ideal condition, and all social relations are regarded as degenerate. The child is to be brought up in isolation by the laws of brute necessity and to have no social or political education until he is fifteen, when an impossible set of expedients for bringing him into touch with his fellows is devised. The absurdity of this anti-social education has always been keenly felt. Children cannot be reared in a social vacuum, nor can they be trained merely as world citizens to the complete exclusion of specific governmental authority. And although society may become stereotyped and corrupt, it yet furnishes the means of carrying the accumulated race experience and attainments. One should remember, however, that the times and the cause had need of just so extreme a doctrine. The reformer is often forced to assume the position of a fanatic, in order to secure attention for his propaganda. Had Rousseau's cry been uttered a generation later, when society had become less artificial and more responsive to popular rights, it might have contained less exaggeration. But at the time such

It is anti-social, but tradition had to be broken, and an extreme doctrine was necessary.

individualism alone could enable him to break the bondage to the past. By means of paradoxes and exaggerations he was able to emphasize the crying need of a natural development of man, and to tear down the effete traditions in educational organization, content, and methods. Moreover, the fallacy involved in such an isolated education is too palpable to deceive any one, and is scarcely sufficient for condemning Rousseau. On the contrary, those who have most admired him and endeavored to develop his theories — Basedow, Pestalozzi, Herbart, and Froebel — have all most insistently stressed social activities in the training of children.

About this position of natural and unsocial education described in the *Emile* cluster several elements of weakness and strength. In the first place, Rousseau is absolutely opposed to all book learning and exaggerates the value of personal observation and inference. He consequently neglects the past, and robs the pupil of all the experience of his fellows and of those who have gone before. But he develops the details of observational and experimental work in elementary training to an extent never previously undertaken, and emphasizes physical activity as a means to the growth and intellectual development of children.

Again, a fact of far greater importance is that, although Rousseau's knowledge of children was exceedingly defec-

It rejects books and the experience of the past, but it develops observation and inference and physical activity.

It fails to understand children, but

tive,[1] and his recommendations were marred by unnatural breaks and filled with sentimentality, he saw the need of studying the child as the only basis for education. In the *Preface to the Emile* he declares: — starts the study of their development, —

"We do not know childhood. Acting on the false ideas we have of it, the farther we go the farther we wander from the right path. The wisest among us are engrossed in what the adult needs to know and fail to consider what children are able to apprehend. We are always looking for the man in the child, without thinking of what he is before he becomes a man. This is the study to which I have devoted myself, to the end that, even though my whole method may be chimerical and false, the reader may still profit by my observations. I may have a very poor conception of what ought to be done, but I think I have the correct view of the subject on which we are to work. Begin, then, by studying your pupils more thoroughly, for assuredly you know nothing about them. Now if you read this book of mine with this purpose in view, I do not believe it will be without profit to you."

As a result of such appeals the child has become the center of discussion in modern training, and we may thank Rousseau for introducing a new principle into education. And, despite his limitations and prejudices, this unnatural and neglectful parent stated many details of child development with much force and clearness and gave an impetus to later reformers, who were able to correct his observations and make them more practicable in education. a new principle in education;

[1] His *Confessions* tell us how he declined to rear his own children, but consigned all five to the public foundling asylum.

and, while dividing the pupil's development into too definite stages, it shows that there are characteristic differences at different stages.

In this connection may be mentioned the sharp division that Rousseau makes of the pupil's development into definite stages that seem but little connected with one another and his prescription of a distinct education for each period. This is often cited as a ruinous breach in the evolution of the individual, and the *reductio ad absurdum* of such an atomic training would seem to be reached in his hope of rendering Emile warm-hearted and pious after keeping him in the meshes of self-interest and doubt until he is fifteen. But such a criticism loses sight of the remarkable contribution to educational theory and practice made thereby. Rousseau has shown that there are characteristic differences at different stages in the child's life, but each 'has a perfection or maturity of its own,' and that only as the proper activities are provided for each stage will it reach that maturity or perfection. It can be seen how these principles fulfill his contention that the child must be studied, and, if put into effect, they would demolish the type of education which then was struggling to introduce the pupil into studies and activities far in advance of his interests and capacities.

Its religion is cold, but lofty; and replaced the traditionalized Christianity and rationalism of the times.

Finally, we should, on the whole, commend Rousseau's religion of nature and deism. While it is lacking in warmth, reality, and power, it did much to replace the institutionalized and dogmatic Christianity, which had been overwhelmed by the attacks of rationalism, with a pure, lofty, and tolerant faith. His mysterious Being penetrating all nature would seem a deity too vague and too removed to be of comfort and refreshment to human souls, but it was sufficient to purify the dying hierarchical system and duly stress the common interests of humanity.

The Influence of Rousseau upon Society and Literature

So revolutionary a work as the *Emile* could hardly escape the wrath of the despotic government and hierarchy. The month following its publication, the Parliament [1] of Paris ordered the book to be burnt and its writer arrested on the charge of irreligion, and shortly afterward the theological doctors of the Sorbonne and the Archbishop of Paris likewise condemned it. Rousseau avoided arrest by fleeing from Montmorency, and from that time until his death was driven from pillar to post, at first by the tyranny of the rulers in Church and State, and later by his own morbid imagination. He would have taken asylum in Geneva, but he found, upon reaching Yverdun, that the Council had closed the gates of his native city to him, and decreed the burning of both the *Emile* and the *Social Contract*. A similar

The Emile was condemned by both the political and the theological authorities, and Rousseau was driven into exile until his death.

---

[1] These local *parlements*, of which that of Paris was the most important, were primarily higher law courts, but, in addition to trying cases, they claimed the right to register or disapprove the decrees of the king, and maintained certain other legislative powers.

persecution met him wherever he went in Switzerland, and in 1766 he fled to England at the invitation of the philosopher Hume. Here he soon imagined himself the victim of a plot, and returned to France, where for more than a decade he wandered about in the vicinity of Paris. In 1778 he died and was buried at Ermenonville. Fifteen years later, during the Reign of Terror, he was hailed as a liberator, and his mortal remains were borne in triumph back to Paris by the revolutionists. There they were laid to rest in the Pantheon, the temple dedicated by France to her greatest sons.

Yet no works have had a wider influence upon society than those of Rousseau.

This recognition was late, but deserved. No other person, indeed, has ever approached Rousseau in pointing out the cares and distresses of the poor and oppressed, as they drag along their existence and produce the prosperity which is concentrated in the hands of a small but privileged group. No works besides his treatises have so graphically depicted the need for a change of front in society, or sounded such a clarion call to the downtrodden to arise in battle. His anarchic and unsocial individualism complemented the rationalism and intellectual skepticism of Voltaire, and there resulted a furious revolution and a blind reaction to the decadent order of society. Rousseau may not have caused the French Revolution, but, as Napoleon declared, it would have been impossible without him. His brilliant and emotional naturalism crystallized the spirit of the times. It furnished the watchwords of the Jacobins and later of the Committee of Public Safety, and shook France from center to circumference. Similarly, America, although inheriting her love of liberty from Anglo-Saxon ancestry, expressed her convictions in formulas taken from the works of Rousseau. The American colonies seem to have assimilated the ideas, phrases, and even words [1] of the Gallic revolutionists and echoed them in the Declaration of Independence, the Articles of Confederation, and in various documents and debates.

In many other ways the influence of Rousseau has been felt. While he has left no direct impress upon the tenets of political science, he has raised many inquiries in that subject that have since had to be answered. He is largely responsible for the conception of socialism and of philosophic anarchy, although his economic writings do not advocate either in specific terms. In religion, the modern tendency to emphasize the emotional element, and at the same time to reject doctrines, ritualism, and extreme organization received an impetus from Rousseau. To him is largely due the development of romanticism in the literature of the late eighteenth and early nineteenth centuries. During that period sentimentality, heroicism, personal adventures, dominance of the emotions, analysis of the passions, and

Rousseau has also indirectly affected political science, theology, and literature.

[1] For example, 'life, liberty, and the pursuit of happiness.'

inner conflicts pervade the writings of France, Germany, England, and America. Likewise, the descriptions of scenery and natural environment, and of the charm of the country, mountains, and lakes in literature, and the love for the natural, picturesque, and rural in art and architecture, largely find their beginnings in Rousseau's naturalism.

His Influence upon Educational Theory and Practice

But he has especially in-fluenced edu-cation in its organization, aim, method, and content.

But the most complete revolution and the most potent effects of Rousselianism appear in educational theory and practice. Few men have had as great an influence upon the organization, method, and content of education. Although his mission was largely to destroy traditionalism, and most of the specific features of his naturalism have in time been modified or rejected, many of the important principles in modern pedagogy go back to him. His criticism caused men to rush to the defense of existing systems, and when they failed in their attempts to reinstate them, they undertook the construction of something better. In the first place, his attitude toward the artificial, superficial, and in-human society of the times led him to oppose its arbi-trary authority and guidance of education according to an unnatural and traditional organization. He advo-cated the virtues of the primitive man and a simpler basis of social organization, and held that all members of society should be trained so as to contribute to their own support and to be sympathetic and benevolent toward their fellows. Through him education has thus been more closely related to human welfare. The present-day emphasis upon the moral aim of education, the cultivation of social virtues, and the development of industrial education alike find some of their roots in the *Emile.* On the side of method and content also, education is indebted to the naturalism of Rousseau. He first insisted upon the study of children as fundamental in education, and showed that the material or activities provided must be in keeping with the different stages of development. Rousseau may, therefore, be credited in part with the modern regard for the freedom of the child and the study of his psychological development. Through him we have come to abandon the conception of the child as only an adult on a small scale. We may thank the *Emile* to some extent, too, for the increasing tendency to cease from forcing upon children a fixed method of thinking, feeling, and acting, and for the gradual disappearance of the old ideas that a task is of educational value according as it is distasteful, and that real education consists in straining to overcome meaningless difficulties.[1] It is likewise due to him primarily that we have recognized the need of physi-

[1] See pp. 63 ff.

cal activities, especially in the earlier development of the child, as a foundation for its growth and learning. Further, it is the education of Emile that suggested familiarity with nature and natural phenomena as a means of counterbalancing the corrupt action of man, and, partly as a result of this, schools and colleges have come to include the study of physical forces, natural environment, plants, and animals.

This is shown by the increase in the works on education since the *Emile* was published;

and by the French 'complaints' and legislation,

The great influence of Rousseau upon education in all its aspects is shown by the library of books since written to contradict, correct, or disseminate his doctrines. During the quarter of a century following the publication of the *Emile*, probably more than twice as many books upon education were published as in the preceding three-quarters of a century. This epoch-making work created and forced a rich harvest of educational thinking for a century after its appearance, and it has affected our ideas upon pedagogical subjects from that day to this. But Rousseau's principles did not take immediate root in the schools themselves, although their influence is manifest there as the nineteenth century advanced. In France they were apparent in the complaints and recommendations concerning schools in many of the *cahiers* [1] that were issued just prior to the Revolution,

---

[1] These were lists of grievances and desired reforms prepared by the various towns and villages throughout France at the request of the king (Louis XVI), in accordance with an old custom.

and afterward clearly formed a basis for much of the legislation concerning the universal, free, and secular organization of educational institutions. In England, since there was no national system of schools, little direct impression was made upon educational practice, but in America this revolutionary thought would seem to have had much to do with causing the unrest that resulted in secularizing and universalizing the public system and in producing the foundation for the first public 'high' schools.[1] The first definite attempt, however, to put into actual practice the naturalistic education of Rousseau occurred in Germany through the writings of Basedow and the foundation of the 'Philanthropinum,' and is of sufficient importance to demand separate discussion in another chapter.

and the American secularization and universalizing of education.

The Revolutionary Nature of Rousseau's Doctrines

It should, however, be noted here that the work of Rousseau was bound up in a revolution from the society, traditions, and education of the past. His theories involved a destruction of the old social and moral sanctions, but did not directly supply much to take their place. A new social order, philosophy, and education were needed to bring about truth and freedom and a reconstructed view of the world. The individual had demanded free sway, and it was now necessary to adjust

Rousseau's doctrines made the reaction to the Middle Ages logically complete.

[1] See Brown, *Making of Our Middle Schools*, Chaps. X and XIII–XIV.

him to his environment without repressing his development. The transition from mediævalism thus became logically complete. It appeared about the middle of the fourteenth century, and, proceeding through a series of interconnected and overlapping advances followed by retrogressions — Renaissance, Reformation, Realism, Puritanism, Pietism, and Rationalism, — reached a genuinely destructive stage in Rousselianism toward the end of the eighteenth century. Evolution had failed, and revolution resulted, but through this was opened the vista of reconstruction on the modern basis.

SUPPLEMENTARY READING

I. Sources

*ROUSSEAU, J. J. *Confessions, Letters,* and *Reveries; Discourse on the Sciences and Arts,* and *Discourse on Inequality; The New Heloise, Social Contract,* and *Emile.*

II. Authorities

BARNARD, H. *American Journal of Education.* Vol. V, pp. 459–486. Or *German Teachers and Educators.* Pp. 459–486.

BROUGHAM, H. *Rousseau (Lives of Men of Letters).*

BROWNING, O. *An Introduction to the History of Educational Theories.* Chap. IX.

BRUNETIÈRE, F. *Manual of the History of French Literature.* (Translated by Derechif.) Pp. 333–414.

CAIRD, C. *Literature and Philosophy.* Vol. I, pp. 105–146.

COMPAYRÉ, G. *History of Pedagogy.* (Translated by Payne.) Chap. XIII.

COMPAYRÉ, G. *Jean Jacques Rousseau and Education from Nature.* (Translated by Jago.)

*DAVIDSON, T. *Rousseau and Education according to Nature.*

FRANCKE, K. *Social Forces in German Literature.* Chaps. VII–VIII.

GIRALDIN, ST. M. *J. J. Rousseau, sa vie et ses ouvrages.*

*HUDSON, W. H. *Rousseau and Naturalism in Life and Thought.*

LANG, O. H. *Rousseau and his Emile.*

LINCOLN, C. H. *Rousseau and the French Revolution (Annals of the American Academy of Political and Social Science,* X, pp. 54–72).

*MACDONALD, F. *Studies in the France of Voltaire and Rousseau.* Chaps. II and VII.

MONROE, P. *Textbook in the History of Education.* Chap. X.

MORIN, S. H. *Life and Character of Rousseau (Littell's Living Age,* XXXVIII, pp. 259–264).

*MORLEY, J. *Rousseau.*

*MUNROE, J. P. *The Educational Ideal.* Chap. VII.

PARKER, S. C. *Our Inherited Practice in Elementary Schools.* II and III (*Elementary School Teacher,* November, 1909, and January, 1910).

QUICK, R. H. *Educational Reformers.* Chap. XIV.

SCHLOSSER, F. C. *History of the Eighteenth Century.* Vols. I and II.

TEXTE, J. *Rousseau and the Cosmopolitan Spirit.* (Translated by Matthews.) Bk. I.

WEIR, S. *The Key to Rousseau's Emile (Educational Review,* V, pp. 278–290).

CHAPTER VIII

BASEDOW AND THE PHILANTHROPINUM

Basedow proved unorthodox in theology and turned to the profession of teaching.

Johann Bernhard Basedow (1723-1790) was by nature the very sort of person to be captivated by Rousseau's doctrines. He was talented but erratic, unorthodox, tactless, and irregular in life. He was the son of a Hamburg wigmaker, but refused to follow his father's business and ran away. A gentleman with whom he took service discovered his remarkable ability and persuaded the lad's father to educate him. After due preparation at home, Basedow was sent to the University of Leipzig for a theological training, but soon proved heretical and again rejected the vocation chosen for him. He then (1749) became a tutor in Holstein to a Herr von Quaalen's children, and with these aristocratic pupils first developed his famous methods of teaching through conversation and play connected with surrounding objects. Within four years his patron secured for him a professorship at the Ritterakademie [1] of Soroe, Denmark, but by 1761 he had given such serious offense by his unorthodox utterances that the government felt obliged to transfer him to the Gymnasium at Altona.

[1] For the nature and development of *Ritterakademien*, see Graves, *History of Education during the Transition*, pp. 290 f.

112

From his position here he flooded Germany with a variety of heretical essays, and was eventually refused the sacrament by the Church.

Basedow's Educational Reforms and Writings

About this time, however, Basedow fell under the spell of Rousseau's *Emile*, which was most congenial to his methods of thinking and teaching, and turned to educational reform. The schools of the day were sadly in need of just such an antidote as naturalism was calculated to furnish. The rooms were dismal and the work unpleasant, physical training was neglected, and the discipline was severe. Children were regarded as adults in miniature, and were so treated both in their dress and their education. The boys had their hair curled, powdered, and smeared with pomade, and wore embroidered coats, dainty knee breeches, silk stockings, and swords. A boy standing by his father would have seemed to differ only in size. Little girls were bound up in whalebone waists, donned enormous hoop skirts, and wore upon their heads "a combination of false curls, puffs, and knots fastened with pins and crowned with plumes." Education was largely a matter of instruction in artificial deportment.[1] The study of classics com-

At the Gymnasium of Altona he was, through the *Emile*, inspired to reform the unnatural education of the day.

[1] For a more complete description of the children's dress of these times and of this 'dancing-master' education, see Parker, *Our Inherited Practice in Elementary Schools* (*Elementary School Teacher*, November, 1909).

I

posed the entire intellectual curriculum, and the methods were purely grammatical.

As a result, Basedow's suggestions for educational improvement attained as great popularity as his theological productions had received abuse. After 1767 he was allowed by Bernstorff, the Minister of Education, to give all his time to reform and yet retain his salary. The following year, in his *Address on Schools and Studies, and their Influence on Public Happiness*, he called generally upon princes, governments, ecclesiastics, and others in power, to assist him in bringing out a work on elementary education, the plan of which was described in outline. The emperor of his native land, the sovereign of his adopted country, and several other rulers of Europe, together with such prominent persons as Bernstorff, Behrisch, Lavater, Goethe, and Kant, showed great interest, and a subsidy to the sum of ten thousand dollars was speedily raised. Six years later, Basedow completed his promised textbook, *Elementarwerk*, and the companion work for teachers and parents known as *Methodenbuch*. The *Elementarwerk* was issued in four volumes with one hundred accompanying plates, which were too large to be bound in with it, and contained many of the principles of Comenius as well as of Rousseau. It has, in fact, been referred to as 'the *Orbis Pictus*[1] of the eighteenth century,' and gives a

[1] See p. 31 for the *Orbis Sensualium Pictus* and its method.

Through his Address on Schools he raised a sufficient subsidy to publish his Elementarwerk and Methodenbuch.

The Elementarwerk contains principles from Comenius as well as Rousseau, and the Methodenbuch does not follow Rousseau literally.

knowledge of things and words in the form of a dialogue. It deals first with natural phenomena and forces, then with morals and the mind, and the method of instruction in natural religion, and finally with social duties, commerce, and affairs. The *Methodenbuch*, while not following Rousseau literally, contains many ideas concerning the natural training of children that are suggestive of him. Later, Basedow, together with Campe, Salzmann, and others of his followers, also produced a series of popular books especially adapted to the character, interests, and needs of children. Of these works, which are all largely filled with didactics, moralizing, religiosity, and scraps of scientific information, the best known is *Robinson der Jüngere*, more often called *Swiss Family Robinson* in America. It seems to have been suggested by Rousseau's recommendation of *Robinson Crusoe* as a textbook,[1] and was published by Campe in 1779.

His followers produced children's books, — among them, Swiss Family Robinson in imitation of Robinson Crusoe.

The Course and Methods of the Philanthropinum

Eight years before this, however, Behrisch had induced Prince Leopold Friedrich Franz to allow Basedow to found at Dessau an educational institution, called the 'Philanthropinum,' which should embody that reformer's ideas. Leopold granted him a salary of eleven hundred

Through Prince Leopold, Basedow founded the 'Philanthropinum' at Dessau, to embody his ideas.

[1] See p. 93.

thalers,[1] and three years later gave him an equipment of buildings, grounds, and endowment. At first Basedow had but three assistants, but later the number was considerably increased. The staff then included several very able men, — such as Wölke, who had taught at Leipzig; Campe, chaplain at Potsdam; Salzmann, who had been a professor at Erfurt; and Matthison, the poet. The attendance at the Philanthropinum was very small in the beginning, since the institution was regarded as an experiment, but eventually the number of pupils rose to more than fifty. They came from many different countries, and the school soon had a wide reputation throughout Europe. After it had been in existence about a year and a half, Basedow invited the scholars and distinguished men from everywhere to attend a great public examination and determine whether the school ought to continue. There are extant two accounts of this inspection, one by Professor Schummel of Magdeburg and the other by Basedow himself, and from these we gain most of our information concerning the institution.

The aim of the school was to direct and not suppress the natural

The underlying principle of the school was "everything according to nature." The natural instincts and interests of the children were only to be directed and not altogether suppressed. They were to be trained as

---

[1] A *thaler* was equivalent to about three shillings, or seventy-three cents.

children and not as adults, and the methods of learning were to be adapted to their stage of mentality. That all of the customary unnaturalness, discomfort, and want of freedom might be eliminated, the boys were plainly dressed in sailor jackets and loose trousers, their collars were turned down and were open at the neck, and their hair was cut short and was free from powder, pomade, and hair bags. *instincts and interests.*

While universal education was believed in, and rich and poor alike were to be trained, it was felt that the natural education of the one class was for social activity and leadership, and of the other for teaching. Consequently, the wealthy boys were to spend six hours in school and two in manual labor, while those from families of small means labored six hours and studied two. Every one, however, was taught handicrafts — carpentry, turning, planing, and threshing — as a recognition of the educative value of constructive work. There were also physical exercises and games for all. On the intellectual side, while Latin was not neglected, more attention was paid to the vernacular and French than to the classics, in order that instruction might deal with realities rather than words. According to the *Elementarwerk*, Basedow planned to create a wide objective and practical course. It was to give some account of man, including bits of anthropology, anatomy, and physiology; of brute creation, especially the uses of domestic *Universal education was advocated, but social distinctions were recognized.*

Every one was given industrial and physical training, Latin was subordinated to modern languages, and a wide objective course was planned.

animals and their relation to industry; of trees and plants, with their growth, culture, and products; of minerals and chemicals; of mathematical and physical instruments; and of trades, history, and commerce. He afterward admitted that he had overestimated the amount of content that was possible for a child, and greatly abridged this material.[1]

Languages were taught by conversation, games, and drawing; arithmetic by mental methods; geometry by drawing; geography by extending out from home; and deism by confining the pupils from nature for a time.

The most striking characteristic of the school, however, was its improved methods. Languages were taught by speaking and then by reading, and grammar was not brought in until late in the course. Facility was acquired through conversation, games, pictures, drawing, acting plays, and reading on practical and interesting subjects. Similar linguistic methods had been recommended by Montaigne, Ratich, and Locke, and largely worked out by Comenius,[2] but were never before made as practical as by Basedow and his assistants. His instruction in arithmetic, geometry, geography, physics, nature study, and history was fully as progressive as that in languages. Arithmetic was taught by mental methods, geometry by drawing figures accurately and neatly, and geography by beginning with one's home, and extending out into the neighborhood, the town, the country, and the continent. In a similarly direct way the pupils were instructed in matters of actual life. For example,

---

[1] The actual program of each day is given in full in Barnard, *German Teachers and Educators*, pp. 519 f.   [2] See pp. 31 and 46.

they cast lots in the classroom to see who should have the privilege of describing the tools and processes of a trade depicted in an engraving. Finally, the Philanthropinic plan for teaching the naturalistic religion of deism should be noted. The boys were prepared for learning of the existence of God by having their attention turned to various features and phenomena of nature and being asked what caused them. Then they were kept in the house for four or five days in a darkened room, so that they would be the more impressed with the wonders of creation when they should be released and told of the God whose handiwork it was.[1]

The Influence of the Philanthropinum

Most visitors to the Philanthropinum were greatly pleased with the institution, especially on account of the interested and alert appearance of the pupils. Kant had such high expectations of its results as to declare in 1777 that it meant "not a slow reform, but a quick revolution," and felt that "by the plan of organization it must of itself throw off all the faults which belong to its beginning." He afterward admitted that he had been too optimistic, but he still felt that the experiment had been well worth while, and had paved the way for better things.

Great expectations were had for the school, and it proved a great stimulus for younger children.

[1] This method of religious education was first practiced by Wölke, but it had been suggested by Basedow in the *Elementarwerk* (Part I, pp. 87–90).

Although it may not have served well for older pupils, it was certainly excellent in its stimulus to children under ten or twelve, who too often are naturally averse to books, and can be captured only by such appeals to the senses and to nature.

The Philanthropinum was soon closed, but similar institutions sprang up throughout Germany, and many new educational ideas arose.

Basedow proved temperamentally unfit to direct the institution. He soon left, and began to teach privately in Dessau and write educational works along the lines he had started. Campe, who first superseded him, withdrew within the year to found a similar school at Hamburg. Institutions of the same type sprang up elsewhere, and some of them had a large influence upon education. In 1793 the Philanthropinum at Dessau was closed permanently, and its teachers were scattered through Germany. Such followers as Wölke, Campe, and Salzmann carried on the Philanthropinic movement with great vigor. On account of its popularity it was adopted by a large number of others, who unfortunately were often mountebanks. They prostituted the system to their own ends, and the profession of teaching was often degraded by them into a mere trade. Nevertheless, the Philanthropinum seems not to have been without good results, especially when we consider the educational conditions and the pedagogy of the times. It introduced many new ideas into all parts of Germany and Switzerland, and these were carefully worked out by such reformers as Pestalozzi, Froebel, and Herbart. Hence, despite his visionary disposition, his intemperance, and his irregularity of living, the reformer who first attempted to embody the valuable aspects of Rousseau's naturalism in the education of Germany was Basedow, rather than Pestalozzi, who afterward transformed it so much more successfully.

SUPPLEMENTARY READING

I. Sources

*Basedow, J. B. *Elementarwerk* and *Methodenbuch*.
Campe, J. H. *Robinson der Jüngere* and *Theorophon*.
Salzmann, C. G. *Conrad Kiefer*.

II. Authorities

*Barnard, H. *German Teachers and Educators*. Pp. 488–520.
*Compayré, G. *History of Pedagogy*. Pp. 414 f.
Garbovicianu, P. *Die Didaktik Basedows im Vergleiche zur Didaktik des Comenius*.
Göring, H. *Ausgewählte Schriften mit Basedows Biographie*.
Lange, O. H. *Basedow: His Educational Work and Principles*.
Payne, J. *Lectures on the History of Education*. Pp. 91–96.
Pinloche, J. A. *Basedow et le Philanthropinisme*.
*Quick, R. H. *Educational Reformers*. Chap. XV.

CHAPTER IX

PESTALOZZI AND EDUCATION AS DEVELOPMENT

THE happiest educational results of Rousseau came through Pestalozzi. Rousseau had shattered the eighteenth-century temple of despotism, privilege, and hypocrisy, but it remained for Pestalozzi to erect a more enduring structure out of the ruins. It was Pestalozzi that developed the negative and inconsistent naturalism of the *Emile* into a positive attempt to reform corrupt society by proper education and a new method of teaching.

The Earlier Life of Pestalozzi

Pestalozzi's early training by his mother influenced his educational ideals, but made him sensitive and unpractical.

But to understand the significance of the experiments, writings, and principles of this widely beloved reformer, one must make a brief study of his life and surroundings. *Johann Heinrich Pestalozzi* was born at Zürich in 1746. Through the death of his father, he was brought up from early childhood almost altogether by his mother. She was a woman of great unselfishness and genuine piety, and her training had a lasting influence upon his educational ideals. From this experience in great measure must have come his later ideas that the home, as a center of love and coöperation, should be a model for the school, and that education should include a training of the heart and hand, as well as of the head, if the race were to be regenerated. Mothers he certainly held to be the ideal teachers, and to them he ever directed his counsel and exhortations. Yet to the maternal guidance must also be ascribed his extraordinary sensibility, imaginativeness, and unpracticality.

Another strong influence upon his life was that of his grandfather, pastor in a neighboring village. Through visits with him to the poor, sick, and distressed of the parish, young Pestalozzi became acquainted with the degradation and suffering of the peasants and resolved to relieve and elevate them. Naturally he first turned to the ministry as being the best way to accomplish this. But he broke down in his trial sermon, and gave up the hope of entering this profession. He then turned to the study of law, with the idea of defending the rights of his people. In this, too, he was destined to be balked; strangely enough, through the influence of Rousseau. In common with several other students of the University of Zürich, he was greatly impressed by the *Social Contract* and the *Emile*, which had recently appeared, and, becoming involved with the rest in a radical criticism of the government, he saw his dreams of public office and useful legislation disappear in thin air.

His grandfather's example inspired him to elevate the peasantry through the ministry, law,

Pestalozzi, accordingly, abandoned his legal career.

improved
agriculture,

Then, in 1769, in the hope of demonstrating to the peasants the value of improved methods of agriculture, he took up, after a year of training, a parcel of waste land at Birr. This he called by the name of *Neuhof* ('new farm'). Within five years the experiment proved a lamentable failure, but even before the final crash Pestalozzi had come to feel that his philanthropy had been absorbed by a material ambition. A son had meantime been born to him, whom he had undertaken to rear upon the basis of the *Emile*, and the results, recorded in a *Father's Journal*, suggested new ideas and educational principles for the regeneration of the masses. He held that education did not consist merely in books and knowledge, and that the children of the poor could, by proper training, be taught to earn their living and at the same time develop their intelligence and moral nature.[1]

His School at Neuhof and the *Leonard and Gertrude*

and philan-
thropic edu-
cation at
Neuhof
(Birr).

Hence the failure of his agricultural venture afforded Pestalozzi the opportunity he craved to experiment with philanthropic education. Toward the end of 1774 he took into his home some twenty of the most needy children he could find. These he fed, clothed, and treated as his own. He gave the boys practical instruction in farming and gardening on small tracts, and had the girls

[1] For a more complete account of his conclusions, see de Guimps, *Pestalozzi*, pp. 75–78.

trained in domestic duties and needlework. In bad weather both sexes gave their time to spinning and weaving cotton. They were also trained in the rudiments, but were practiced in conversing and in memorizing the Bible before learning to read and write. The scholastic instruction was given very largely while they were working, and, although Pestalozzi had not as yet learned to make any direct connection between the occupational and the formal elements, this first attempt at an industrial education made it evident that the two could be combined. Within a few months there was a striking improvement in the physique, minds, and morals of the children, as well as in the use of their hands. But Pestalozzi was so enthusiastic over the success of his experiment that he greatly increased the number of children, and by 1780 was reduced to bankruptcy.

Nevertheless, his wider purpose of social reform by means of education was not allowed to languish altogether, for a friend [1] shortly persuaded him to publish his views. The *Evening Hour of a Hermit*,[2] a collection of one hundred and eighty aphorisms, was his first production. This work contained, as von Raumer puts it, "the fruit of Pestalozzi's past years and at the same time

When his educational experiment was closed, he wrote out his views in a series of works, of which Leonard and Gertrude alone proved popular.

---

[1] Iselin, the editor of *Ephemerides*.

[2] *Die Abendstunde eines Einsiedlers.* A translation of the entire work can be found in Barnard, Vol. VI, pp. 169–179, while its essence is given by de Guimps, *Pestalozzi*, pp. 75–78.

the seed corn of the years that were to come, — the plan
and key to his action in pedagogy," but it could be understood by few of the people and received little attention.
Pestalozzi was, therefore, advised to put his thought into
more popular form, and in 1781 he wrote his well-known
story of *Leonard and Gertrude*.[1]   This work, with the subsequent additions,[2] gives an account of the degraded
social conditions in the Swiss village of 'Bonnal' and the
changes wrought in them by one simple peasant woman.
'Gertrude' reforms her drunkard husband, educates her
children, and causes the whole community to feel her
influence and adopt her methods.   When finally a wise
schoolmaster comes to the village, he learns from Gertrude the proper conduct of the school and begs for her
continued coöperation.   Then the government becomes
interested, studies the improvements that have taken
place, and concludes that the whole country can be re-

[1] *Lienhard und Gertrud: ein Buch für das Volk.*

[2] To elucidate more fully the teachings of this story, the following year
Pestalozzi wrote his *Christopher and Eliza*, and to show how it could be
used as a manual of popular education, he later produced *The Instruction
of Children in the Home*, and *Figures to my A B C Book* (afterward called
Fables), but the public, wishing only to be amused, would not read them,
and Pestalozzi was driven by popular taste to add other parts to the *Leonard and Gertrude* in 1783, 1785, and 1787.   A translation of the original
first volume, with excerpts from the later parts concerning the village
school, is given in Barnard, *American Journal of Education*, Vol. VII,
pp. 525–648.   An admirable condensation of the whole work has been
made by Eva Channing (Boston, 1892).

formed in no better way than by imitating Bonnal. The *Leonard and Gertrude* appealed especially to the romanticism of the period, and constituted Pestalozzi's one popular success in literature. It was, however, taken simply as an interesting story, and the author's suggestions for social, political, and educational reform were generally passed over.[1]

His School at Stanz and the Observational Methods

During the last decade of his life at Neuhof, Pestalozzi was too busy warding off poverty and starvation to write or develop his principles. But in 1798 a turn in political fortunes gave him another opportunity to test his theories by actual practice. In that year Switzerland came under the control of the French revolutionists, and the independent cantons were united in a Helvetic Republic under a 'directorate' like that in France. As this movement promised reform, Pestalozzi enthusiastically supported it. He was in turn offered patronage by the new government, but he asked only for a school in which he might carry out his principles. While the authorities were settling upon a site near his home, an unexpected occurrence brought him instead to the village of Stanz. The Catholic community in this place had refused to

At fifty-two he took charge of a throng of orphan children in the Ursuline convent at Stanz.

[1] See footnote 2 on p. 126. His attempt to formulate his views in a thoroughly philosophical way by his *Inquiry into the Course of Nature in the Development of the Human Race* must have met with very little success.

yield to what they considered a foreign and atheistic invasion, and most of the able-bodied adults had been slaughtered. That left the government with a throng of friendless children for whom they felt bound to provide. Pestalozzi, being asked to take charge of them, started an orphan home and school in the Ursuline convent at Stanz. Here he soon gained the confidence and love of the children, and produced a most noticeable improvement in them physically, morally, and intellectually.

Through experience and observation, rather than books, he taught the children morality and religion,

He declined all assistants, books, and materials, as he felt that none of the conventional methods could be of service in his work, and he sought to instruct the children rather by experience and observation than by abstract statements and words. Religion and morals, for example, were never taught by precepts, but through instances that arose in their own lives he showed them the value of self-control, charity, sympathy, and gratitude. To a friend he declared : —

"I strove to awaken the feeling of each virtue before talking about it, for I thought it unwise to talk to children on subjects which would compel them to speak without thoroughly understanding what they were saying." [1]

number, language, geography, history, and natural history.

In a similarly concrete way the pupils were instructed in number and language work by means of objects, and in geography and history by conversation rather than by

[1] See *How Gertrude Teaches Her Children*, I.

books. While they did not learn their natural history primarily from nature, they were taught to corroborate what they had learned by their own observation. With regard to this whole method Pestalozzi said : —

"I believe that the first development of thought in the child is very much disturbed by a wordy system of teaching, which is not adapted either to his faculties or the circumstances of his life. According to my experience, success depends upon whether what is taught to children commends itself to them as true through being closely connected with their own observation. As a general rule, I attached little importance to the study of words, even when explanations of the ideas they represented were given." [1]

In connection with his observational method, Pestalozzi at this time began his attempts to reduce all observation to its lowest terms.[2] It was while at Stanz, for example, that he first adopted his well-known plan of teaching children to read by means of exercises known as 'syllabaries.' These joined the five vowels in succession to the different consonants, — 'ab, eb, ib, ob, ub,' and so on through all the consonants. From the phonetic nature of German spelling, he was able to make the exercises very simple, and intended thus to furnish a necessary practice in basal syllables. In a similar way he hoped to simplify all education to such an extent that

He sought to reduce observation to its lowest terms, as, for example, in his 'syllabaries';

----

[1] See footnote on p. 128.

[2] The resulting elements he soon came to call the 'A B C of observation' (A B C der Anschauung). See pp. 133 and 135.

K

schools would eventually become unnecessary, and that each mother would be able to teach her children and continue her own education at the same time. Moreover, while not altogether successful in his efforts at a correlation, Pestalozzi, more than at Neuhof, now "sought to combine study with manual labor, the school with the workshop," for, said he : —

and to combine study with manual labor.

"I am more than ever convinced that as soon as we have educational establishments combined with workshops, and conducted on a truly psychological basis, a generation will necessarily be formed which will show us by experience that our present studies do not require one tenth of the time or trouble we now give to them."

The 'Institute' at Burgdorf and the Psychologizing of Education

Being forced to give up at Stanz, he obtained with difficulty a position at Burgdorf,

From these methods and principles that Pestalozzi started at Stanz eventually developed all his educational contributions. But before the close of a year the convent that had served as such a fruitful experiment station was required by the French soldiers for a hospital. As soon as he recovered from the terrific physical strain under which he had labored, Pestalozzi was forced to seek another place in which to continue his educational work. But, according to the usual standards for securing a position to teach, "he had everything against him; thick, indistinct speech, bad writing, ignorance of drawing, scorn of grammatical learning. He had studied various branches of natural history, but without any particular attention either to classification or terminology. He was conversant with the ordinary numerical operations, but he would have had difficulty to get through a really long sum in multiplication or division, and had probably never tried to work out a problem in geometry."[1] And in spite of his understanding of "the mind of man and the laws of its development, human affections, and the art of arousing and ennobling them,"[1] he would probably have been unable to obtain a school, had it not been for certain influential friends in the town of Burgdorf. They secured a position for him, first in the school for the tenants and poorer people, and later in the elementary school of the citizens.

In Burgdorf, Pestalozzi "followed without any plan the empirical method interrupted at Stanz," and "sought by every means to bring the elements of reading and arithmetic to the greatest simplicity, and by grouping them psychologically, enable the child to pass easily and surely from the first step to the second, and from the second to the third, and so on."[2] He further worked out and graduated his 'syllabaries,' and invented the idea of large movable letters for teaching the children to read. Language exercises were given his pupils by means of examining the number, form, position, and color of the designs,

where he continued and developed his method.

He taught reading through the 'syllabaries,' language through objects, arithmetic through the 'table of

[1] Charles Monnard, *Histoire de la Suisse, continuation de Müller.*
[2] See footnote on p. 128.

units,' and
geometry
through
drawing
lines and
curves;

holes, and rents in the wall paper of the school,[1] and expressing their observations in longer and longer sentences, which they repeated after him.   For arithmetic he devised boards divided into squares upon which were placed dots or lines concretely representing each unit up to one hundred.   By means of this 'table of units'[2] the pupil obtained a clear idea of the meaning of the digits and the process of addition, and practiced his knowledge further by counting his fingers, beans, pebbles, and other objects. Pestalozzi further explained that "after the child has come to a full understanding of the combinations of units up to ten, and has learned to express himself with ease, the objects are again presented, but the questions are changed : ' If we have two objects, how many times one object ? '   The child looks, counts, and answers correctly." In that way the pupils learned to multiply, and the meaning of division and subtraction was similarly acquired. The children were also taught the elements of geometry by drawing angles, lines, and curves.   Likewise, the development of teaching history, geography, and natural history by this method of observation must have been continued at Burgdorf.

[1] In the *Book for Mothers*, the human body, with its parts and relations, is especially suggested as the material for conversation, since this is the closest to human interests and thought.

[2] An illustration of this table is given in Krüsi, *Pestalozzi*, p. 172.   This system was probably not completed until Pestalozzi settled at Yverdun, and much of the credit for the scheme should go to Krüsi and Schmid.

As a result of these experiments, says Pestalozzi, "there unfolded itself gradually in my mind the idea of the possibility of an A B C of observation,[1] to which I now attach great importance, and with the working out of which the whole scheme of a general method of instruction in all its scope appeared, though still obscure, before my eyes." [2]   And the underlying principle of his system he shortly formulated most tersely in the statement, "I wish to psychologize education." [3]   By this, he showed, is meant the harmonizing of instruction with the laws of intellectual development, together with the simplification of the elements of knowledge and their reduction to a series of exercises so scientifically graded that even the lowest classes can obtain the proper physical, mental, and moral development.   And sense perception or observation, he holds, when connected with language for expressing the different impressions, is, therefore, the foundation of education.

and thus evolved his 'A B C of observation,' and his stated wish to 'psychologize education.'

Despite a want of system and errors in carrying out his method, Pestalozzi seems to have produced remarkable results from the start.   At the first annual examination the Burgdorf School Commission wrote him that

Pestalozzi's 'institute' at Burgdorf was immensely successful, — pupils

---

[1] See footnote 2 on p. 129.   Cf. also footnote 2 on p. 135.

[2] See footnote on p. 128.

[3] *Ich will den menschlichen Unterricht psychologisieren.*   This formula was made by him when asked for a written statement of his system by the 'Friends of Education,' a society that was striving to propagate his views.

poured in, progressive teachers came to assist him, and distinguished visitors flocked there

"the surprising progress of your little scholars of various capacities shows plainly that every one is good for something, if the teacher knows how to get at his abilities and develop them according to the laws of psychology." And the reformer soon met with even greater success in a school of his own. In January, 1801, the government granted him the free use of the 'castle,' or town hall, of Burgdorf and a small subsidy for his 'institute.' Pupils poured in; a number of progressive teachers, including Krüsi, Tobler, Buss, and Niederer,[1] came to assist him; many persons of prominence visited the school and made most favorable reports upon its methods; and during the following three years and a half the Pestalozzian views on education were systematically developed and applied.

How Gertrude Teaches Her Children and Other Works

Pestalozzi was also able at Burgdorf to undertake a detailed statement of his method by the publication in Octo-

[1] Hermann Krüsi, a young schoolmaster of Gais, had, during a famine in Appenzell, brought a troop of starving children to Burgdorf at the invitation of Fischer, a friend of Pestalozzi. Fischer died shortly afterward, and Krüsi joined Pestalozzi's venture. Through Krüsi, the services of Tobler, "a private tutor whose youth had been much neglected," and of Buss, "a bookbinder, who devoted his leisure to singing and drawing," were also secured for the institute. Niederer was a clergyman and philosopher, who gave up his parochial duties to work with Pestalozzi.

ber, 1801, of his *How Gertrude Teaches Her Children*.[1] This work does not mention Gertrude, but consists of fifteen letters to his friend, Gessner. The first two letters contain biographical details, especially concerning the meeting with his assistant teachers. Then follows an account of his general principles; of the specific teaching of language, drawing, writing, measuring, and number by means of observation; of the elementary books that he contemplates writing, — the *A B C of Observation* and the *Book for Mothers;* [2] of the reform in elementary education and of the need of judgment as well as knowledge; and of moral and religious development. Like all of Pestalozzi's works, *How Gertrude Teaches Her Children* is quite lacking in both plan and proportion, and is filled with repetitions and digressions. It contains, however, the foundation of his system and of most modern reform in elementary education, and has to be studied to reveal its values. It has already been quoted several times directly, but the following summary of its principles, made by Pestalozzi's biographer, Morf, after a most care-

To explain his method in detail, he wrote *How Gertrude Teaches Her Children*.

----

[1] *Wie Gertrud ihre Kinder lehrt.*

[2] *A B C der Anschauung* and *Buch der Mütter.* The *Book for Mothers* was later written under Pestalozzi's direction at Burgdorf by Krüsi. It completely failed in its purpose, however, since the average mother was unable to break from the ideals and habits of her own schooldays. The *A B C of Observation* also appeared, and during this period Pestalozzi and his assistants likewise produced a variety of books applying the new method to various school subjects.

ful study of this unsystematic work, may serve to give an idea of Pestalozzi's educational creed. He had come to believe : —

"1. Observation is the foundation of instruction.

"2. Language must be connected with observation.

"3. The time for learning is not the time for judgment and criticism.

"4. In each branch, instruction must begin with the simplest elements, and proceed gradually by following the child's development; that is, by a series of steps which are psychologically connected.

"5. A pause must be made at each stage of the instruction sufficiently long for the child to get the new matter thoroughly into his grasp and under his control.

"6. Teaching must follow the path of development, and not that of dogmatic exposition.

"7. The individuality of the pupil must be sacred for the teacher.

"8. The chief aim of elementary instruction is not to furnish the child with knowledge and talents, but to develop and increase the powers of his mind.

"9. To knowledge must be joined power; to what is known, the ability to turn it to account.

"10. The relations between master and pupil, especially so far as discipline is concerned, must be established and regulated by love.

"11. Instruction must be subordinated to the higher end of education."

Pestalozzi's Attempted Union with Fellenberg

While this productive work at Burgdorf was at its height, a change in the political situation overthrew everything. In 1804 the cantonal government demanded back the 'castle,' although it turned over to Pestalozzi an old convent at Münchenbuchsee. For a few months the reformer made a fruitless attempt to coöperate in his new location with *Emanuel von Fellenberg* (1771–1844), who had founded in the neighboring Hofwyl a prosperous industrial school upon Pestalozzian principles. This school of Fellenberg has played so important a part in American educational history as to deserve more extended consideration than can be given here. The founder had, from his early youth, felt a great sympathy for the poor and unfortunate, and when, while holding an important government office, he came to despair of ever accomplishing anything by legislation, he turned his attention directly to practical educational reform. He purchased an estate at Hofwyl,[1] and started industrial training on the basis of Pestalozzi's experiences, with which he had long been acquainted. Owing to his ability as an organizer and administrator, his school was conducted with ever increasing success from 1804 until his death. He was careful to introduce the various features of his work gradually. Believing that agriculture, as the chief industry of the country, would afford the most effective physical and intellectual training, he

---

[1] It is said that the name of the estate had been Wylhof, but that Fellenberg inverted the syllables to indicate the radical nature of his reforms.

laid out a farm of some six hundred acres, and, with the addition of the necessary workshops, undertook to train farm laborers, cartmakers, blacksmiths, carpenters, locksmiths, shoemakers, and tailors. This 'Agricultural Institute' furnished a practical training for the poor and enabled them to support themselves by their labor while being educated. Through the same institution he also undertook to train rural school-teachers. But his work did not stop there. He felt that the wealthy should understand and be more in sympathy with the laboring classes, and learn how to direct their work intelligently. Accordingly, he established on the estate a 'Literary Institute,' with the usual classical course for the boys of the upper classes. Both sets of boys had to cultivate gardens and work on the farm, and in many other ways come into touch and mutual understanding.

The 'Institute' at Yverdun and the Culmination of the Pestalozzian Methods

Pestalozzi transferred his 'institute' to Yverdun, where his success was greater than ever.

When, however, despite their similarity of purpose, a marked difference of temperaments made a union of the work of Pestalozzi and Fellenberg impossible, Pestalozzi transferred his school to Yverdun in 1805, and was soon followed by most of his assistants. The 'institute' here sprang into fame almost immediately, and increased in numbers and prosperity for several years. Children were sent to Yverdun from great distances, and teachers

thronged here to·learn and apply the new principles at
home. Visitors and sightseers came from all parts of
Europe and America. Pestalozzi was decorated by the
Czar of Russia, and presented with distinctions from
other monarchs. A flourishing girls' school grew up
near the institute under the direction of associates, and
for a short time Pestalozzi himself conducted a school
for orphans in the neighborhood, while Conrad Naef of
Zürich came to Yverdun and founded a celebrated institution for the deaf and dumb upon the Pestalozzian
principles.

The work of the institute at Yverdun was a continuation and culmination of that started at Stanz and Burgdorf. It was a great center of educational experimentation, and nearly every advanced method characteristic of
present elementary education was first undertaken there.
The keynote in teaching all subjects was observation
connected with language. The children were taught to
observe correctly and form the right idea of the relations
of things, and so to have no difficulty in expressing clearly
what they thoroughly understood. The simplification
introduced through the 'syllabaries' and 'table of units'
was further elaborated. A 'table of fractions' was also
devised for teaching that subject concretely. It consisted of a series of squares, which could be divided in-
definitely and in different ways. Some of the squares
were whole, while others were divided horizontally into

Here he
elaborated
the 'sylla-
baries' and
'table of
units,' and
added the
'table of
fractions'
and the
'table of
fractions of
fractions';

two, three, or even ten equal parts. The pupil thus learned by observation to count the parts of units and form them into integers. There was further developed a 'table of fractions of fractions,' or compound fractions,[1] in which the squares were divided, not only horizontally, but vertically, so that the method of reducing two fractions to the same denominator might be self-evident. It was in this number work that the Pestalozzians were most radical. By means of various devices Krüsi, and afterward Schmid [2] even more, attained great clearness, accuracy, and rapidity in arithmetic. The work was often done aloud without paper, and many of the students became most apt in calculation.

drawing, writing, and geometry were taught through elements of form taken from objects;

Similarly, in order to draw and write, the pupil was first taught the simple elements of form. The consecutive exercises for building up form from its elements, however, Pestalozzi was not happy in determining, but Buss successfully worked out an 'alphabet of form.' Objects, such as sticks or pencils, were placed in different directions, and lines representing them were drawn on the board or slate until all elementary forms, straight or curved, were mastered. The pupils combined these elements, instead of copying

---

[1] This table can be found in the Holland, Turner, and Cooke edition (Syracuse, 1898) of *How Gertrude Teaches Her Children*, p. 217.

[2] Joseph Schmid was a Tyrolese shepherd boy, who had first come to Yverdun as a pupil, but because of his brilliancy was soon promoted to be an assistant master.

models, and were encouraged to design symmetrical and graceful figures. This also paved the way for writing, for, said Pestalozzi, "In endeavoring to teach writing, I found I must begin by teaching drawing." The children wrote on their slates, beginning with the easiest letters and gradually forming words from them, but soon learned to write on paper with a pen. Writing was, however, taught in connection with reading, although begun somewhat later than that study. Constructive geometry was also learned through drawing. Much use was made of squares, which were divided into smaller squares or rectangles, and thus sense impression preparatory to geometry was furnished. The pupils were taught to distinguish, first vertical, horizontal, oblique, and parallel lines; then they learned right, acute, and obtuse angles, different kinds of triangles, quadrilaterals, and other figures; and finally discovered at how many points a certain number of straight lines may be made to cut one another, and how many angles, triangles, and quadrilaterals can be formed. To make the matter more concrete the figures were often cut out of cardboard or made into models. Thus the pupils were led up to theoretical geometry, which was made more valuable and interesting by their working out the demonstrations for themselves, instead of learning them from a book.

In nature study, geography, and history the concrete observational work was similarly continued. Trees, _{natural science and}

geography from actual observation; music from its simplest tone elements; and religion and morality from concrete examples.

flowers, and birds were viewed, drawn, and discussed. The pupils began in geography by acquiring the points of the compass and relative positions, and from this knowledge observed and described some familiar place. The valley of the Buron near at hand was observed in detail and modeled upon long tables in clay brought from its sides.   Then the pupils were shown the map for the first time and easily grasped the meaning of its symbols.   Pestalozzi himself did not altogether understand the real purpose of geography, regarding it rather as a means for cultivating language, but he inspired some of his assistants, like Tobler and Ritter, with a great love for the subject and a desire to work it out psychologically. Nor was Pestalozzi sufficiently acquainted with music to apply his method to it.   This was, however, done by his friend, Nägeli, a Swiss composer of note, who reduced it to its simplest elements and then combined and developed these progressively into more complex and connected wholes.   Pupils were thus led to discover pleasing combinations and develop musical inventiveness.   In religious and moral training, as at Stanz, Pestalozzi sought by concrete examples to quicken the germ of conscience into action and develop it by successive steps. The love of God he believed could be taught better through the child's love for his mother [1] and other human

[1] See *How Gertrude Teaches Her Children*, XIV and XV.

beings than through dogma and catechism, and the significance of obedience, duty, and unselfishness through being required to wait before having his desires fulfilled, and so realizing that his own is not the only will or pleasure in the world.

During this period, also, many books upon the applications of the new methods were issued both by Pestalozzi and his assistants. The most famous was probably Schmid's *Exercises on Numbers and Forms*. Niederer also undertook to put the doctrines of Pestalozzi into philosophic form, and published several treatises and pamphlets. A *Weekly Journal* was likewise issued for several years, and a complete edition of Pestalozzi's works was brought out.

Many books upon the new methods were issued.

With all these achievements, however, the institute of Yverdun was slowly dying. Pestalozzi was never a practical administrator, and he was now an old man. The death of his wife deprived him of most of the mental balance that remained to him. He came to depend almost entirely upon his assistant, Schmid, who was most despotic and drove away several of the best teachers from the institute. Disputes and lawsuits became common, and the finances of the institution went from bad to worse. The constant interruptions of visitors also demoralized the school. Finally, in 1825, after an existence of a score of years and with a reputation throughout the civilized world, the institute was closed. Pesta-

But, owing to his own unpracticality, the internal dissensions, and the interruptions from visitors, the institute at Yverdun closed after existing a score of years, and Pestalozzi died two years later.

lozzi retired to Neuhof, then in possession of his grandson. Two years later he died and was buried near his old home beside the school of the little village.[1]

Pestalozzi's Educational Aim

Pestalozzi makes explicit Rousseau's 'naturalism' by defining education as a natural development of human capacities, and contrasting this with the formal education of the day.

After this account of Pestalozzi's personality, experiments, and writings, we are ready to discuss his aim in education and to understand in what sense his principles were a continuation of Rousseau's 'naturalism.' In his first writing, *The Evening Hour of a Hermit*, he held that "all the beneficent powers of man are due to neither art nor chance, but to nature," and that education should follow "the course laid down by nature." So in all his works he constantly returns to the analogy of the child's development with that of the natural growth of the plant or animal. For example, he writes : —

"Sound education stands before me symbolized by a tree planted near fertilizing waters. A little seed, which contains the design of the tree, its form and proportions, is placed in the soil. See how it germinates and expands into trunk, branches, leaves, flowers, and fruit. The whole tree is an uninterrupted chain of organic parts, the plan of which existed in its seed and root. Man is similar to the tree. In the new-born child are hidden those faculties which are to unfold during life. The individual and separate organs of his being form themselves gradually into unison, and build up humanity in the image of God."

[1] A memorial inscription, which now covers the rear of the schoolhouse, after relating his labors and achievements, closes with these fitting words : " Man, Christian, citizen. Everything for others, nothing for self. Blessings on his name."

Consequently, Pestalozzi defines education as "the natural, progressive, and harmonious development of all the powers and capacities of the human being," and insists that "the knowledge to which the child is to be led by instruction must, therefore, be subjected to a certain order of succession, the beginning of which must be adapted to the first unfolding of his powers, and the progress kept exactly parallel to that of his development." In contrast to this education in harmony with nature, Pestalozzi saw that the traditional practices of the times gave the pupil a mere ability to read words, a memory knowledge of mathematics, and a superficial culture through the classics that was purely formal and ineffective for real development. "Our unpsychological schools," he declares, "are essentially only artificial stifling machines for destroying all the results of the power and experience that nature herself brings to life. . . . After the children have enjoyed the happiness of sensuous life for five whole years, we make all nature around them vanish before their eyes; tyrannically stop the delightful course of their unrestrained freedom; pen them up like sheep, whole flocks huddled together in stinking rooms; pitilessly chain them for hours, days, weeks, months, years, to the contemplation of unnatural and unattractive letters, and, contrasted with their former condition, to a maddening course of life."

This need for gradually developing the powers of the

L

child in keeping with nature and the complete absence of it in the schools of the period had been pointed out by Rousseau, but in a purely destructive way.   He talked blindly in his 'naturalism' about an abandonment of all society and civilization and a return to nature, but he failed to make his educational doctrine concrete and explicit and to apply it to the school.   Pestalozzi further modified and extended the Rousselian doctrine by recommending its application to all children, whatever their circumstances and abilities.   Where Rousseau evidently had only the young aristocrat in mind in the education of *Emile*, Pestalozzi held that poverty could be relieved and society reformed only through ridding each and every one of his degradation by means of mental and moral development.   Accordingly, he was the stanch advocate of universal education, as shown by the protest implied in the following simile : —

He further extended Rousselianism by applying it to all children.

"As far as I am acquainted with popular instruction, it appears to me like a large house, whose uppermost story shines in splendor of highly finished art, but is occupied by only a few.   In the middle story is a great crowd, but the stairs by which the upper one may be reached in an approved and respectable manner are wanting; if the attempt be made in a less regular way, the leg or arm used as a means of progress may be broken.   In the lowest story is an immense throng of people, who have precisely the same right to enjoy the light of the sun as those in the upper one; but they are left in utter darkness and not even allowed to gaze at the magnificence above."

His General Method and Its Applications

Pestalozzi's underlying principle for producing this natural development of the powers of all and so for reforming social conditions was to train his pupils in 'observation.'[1] He felt that clear ideas could be formed only through careful sense perceptions, and was thoroughly opposed to the mechanical memorizing with little understanding that was current in the schools of the day. In all studies, therefore, he strove to direct the senses of the pupils to outer objects and to arouse their consciousness by the impressions thus produced. While such 'object lessons' did not exist in the traditionalized schools, Pestalozzi insisted that the material for them is all about the children, and that it can best be obtained in the home and school and in the ordinary occupations, surroundings, and experiences of life. His method in general seems to have been to analyze each subject into its simplest elements and to develop it by graded exercises based as far as possible upon the study of objects rather than words. Yet Pestalozzi felt that "experiences must be clearly expressed in words, or otherwise there arises the same danger that characterizes the dominant word teaching, — that of attributing entirely erroneous ideas to words." Accordingly, as shown in the summary of *How Gertrude Teaches Her Children*,[2] in all instruction he would connect language with observation.

His general method was training in 'observation' through the surrounding material, analysis into its simplest elements, and expression in words.

[1] I.e. *Anschauung.*　　　　　　　[2] See p. 136.

This received special applications to language, arithmetic, drawing, writing, geometry, geography, and other subjects of the curriculum.

The application of this method of natural development by means of analysis, observation, and expression to the various studies constituted the most far-reaching work of Pestalozzi. The special applications of this general method that were worked out by him and his followers in the most common subjects of the curriculum have been described in detail in the account of his work at Stanz, Burgdorf, and Yverdun. Language was taught, not by abstract rules, but by conversation concerning objects. As thinking is thus made to precede language, speaking is held to precede grammar, reading, spelling, and composition. The language training began with single elements or sounds, learned through the 'syllabaries'; from these words were built up; and from words, sentences. As sounds were the elements in language, numbers were the basis of arithmetic. Here again observation was used, and numbers and their relations were taught the pupil through objects. For this purpose the various tables of units, fractions, and compound fractions were devised. Similarly, from the rudiments of form were taught drawing, writing, and constructive and theoretical geometry. For the study of geography, nature, and history, elements were found in the locality that could be combined until the whole world and all the relations of man were worked out. Music was reduced to its simplest elements and progressively developed, and moral and religious training was given through the ordinary concrete relations and experiences of life.

The discipline connected with Pestalozzi's method was naturally mild. Throughout his work he maintained that the school should be as nearly like the home as possible, and that the chief incentives to right are not fear, but kindness and love. In such a sympathetic atmosphere, where the pupils were constantly busied with interesting activities, and all their physical, intellectual, and moral needs were regarded, it is not remarkable that severe punishment was seldom required. On this point Pestalozzi most sensibly remarks: —

His discipline was mild.

> "I do not venture to assert that corporal punishment is inadmissible, but I do object to its application when the teacher or the method is at fault and not the children."

The Permanent Influence of His Principles

It is easy to exaggerate the achievements of this almost sainted reformer of Switzerland. Pestalozzi's doctrines were neither very original nor well carried out. His merit lay in making concrete and positive the abstract and general principles of Rousseau, and in applying them to the schools. Even in this he somewhat failed in practicality and consistency. He was often unable to apply his own method; he grasped principles, but not details. While he stated his views in general most convincingly, we have seen that much

Pestalozzi was neither very original nor consistent in his doctrines, had to be worked out by his assistants and followers. This he realized when he declared : —

"I cannot say that it is I who have created what you see before you now. Niederer, Krüsi, and Schmid would laugh if I called myself their master. I am good neither at figures nor writing; I know nothing about grammar, mathematics, or any other science; the most ignorant of our pupils knows more of these things than I do. I am but the initiative of the institute and depend upon others to carry out my views."

Often he badly violated his own principles. Although strongly opposed to all verbal and *memoriter* teaching, in language work he made the mistake of shaping the sentences for his pupils and having them repeat after him; he insisted upon teaching reading and spelling by pronouncing every possible variety of syllable; and in geography, history, and nature study he required the pupils to commit mere lists of important places, facts, or objects arranged in alphabetic order.

and was often repetitious, inaccurate, and lacking in comprehensiveness.

Moreover, as can be seen both in his educational experiments and his writings, Pestalozzi was groping and never possessed full insight. His works are poorly arranged, repetitious, and inaccurate. There was little organization or order in his schools. Toward the close of his life, he modestly confessed : —

"Poor, weak, humble, unworthy, incapable, and ignorant, I yet set myself to my work. The world accounted it madness, but God's hand was with me. My work prospered. I found friends who loved both it and me. I knew not what I did, I hardly knew what I wanted. And yet my work prospered."

The inconsistency and incompleteness of Pestalozzi's work, however, is of small import when compared with its influence upon society and education. The value of his achievements rests, not in their adequacy or finality, but in the fact that they were the germ of all modern pedagogy and reform. In the eighteenth century caste ruled through wealth and education, while the masses, who supported the owners of the land in idleness and luxury, were sunk in ignorance, poverty, and vice. The schools for the common people were exceedingly few, the content of education was largely limited by ecclesiastical authority, and the methods were traditional and verbal. Brutal discipline and corporal punishment accompanied the *memoriter* methods. The teachers generally had received little training, and were selected at random. Often it was only the old soldier, widow, servant, or workman who gathered the children for an hour or two on Sundays to learn the rudiments. Ordinarily the pay was wretched, no lodgings were provided for the teacher, and he had often to add domestic service to his duties, in order to secure food and clothing.

But his principles furnished the germ of modern pedagogy and educational reform.

In the midst of such conditions appeared this Swiss reformer and most famous of modern educators, who never ceased to work for the reformation of society through education. He saw what education might do to purify social conditions and to elevate the people,

He held education to be a panacea for all social ills.

and attempted to apply it. As Voltaire, Rousseau, and others had held that the panacea for the corrupt times was rationalism, atheism, deism, socialism, anarchy, or individualism, Pestalozzi found his remedy in education. Like Rousseau, he keenly felt the injustice, unnaturalness, and degradation of the existing society, but he was not content to stop with mere destruction and negations. He saw what education might do to purify social conditions and to elevate the people, and he burned to apply it universally and to develop methods in keeping with nature. He would make Rousseau's naturalism specific and extend it to all.

His example, with that of Fellenberg, suggested various types of industrial education.

Hence through Pestalozzi has gradually been strengthened the demand for universal popular education. Through his example at Neuhof and Stanz, and still more through the model institutions of his practical disciple, Fellenberg, at Hofwyl, various types of industrial education have come to supplement the academic courses, and extend the work of the school to a larger number of pupils. The poor, the defective, and the degraded have, through his efforts, been redeemed and given an opportunity in life, and many children have been kept in school that would inevitably have fallen by the wayside. Public schools, special industrial schools, orphanages, institutions for the deaf and blind, reformatories, and even prisons have thus yielded rich harvests because of his first sowing. Likewise, the tendency of modern society to care for the education of the unfortunate through industrial training has sprung from the philanthropic spirit of Pestalozzi and his endeavors to furnish educational opportunities for all.

The efforts of Pestalozzi to evolve a natural method of teaching were likewise fruitful. Through his experiments, educational theory has come, in place of formal principles and traditional processes, to work out carefully and patiently the development of the child mind and to embody the results in practice. And, above all, Pestalozzi's work has made clear the new spirit in the school by which it has approached the atmosphere of the home. He found the proper relation of pupil and teacher to exist in sympathy and friendship, or, as he states it, in 'love.' This attitude constituted the greatest contrast to that of the brutal schools of the times and introduced a new conception into education.

His natural method has replaced the old formal principles, and caused the school to approach the sympathy of the home.

What, then, if Pestalozzi be right in saying, "My life has produced nothing whole, nothing complete; my work cannot, then, either be a whole, nor complete"? If he never produced a closed and perfected system, so much the better. It is not merely the form of his experiments nor even the results, but the fact that he believed in finding his theory through experiment, and not tradition, that made the work of Pestalozzi suggestive and fruitful afterward. In fact, whenever his practice was most fixed, it was least effective; and

If his system was not closed and perfected, it was for that reason the more effective.

wherever his spirit has since prevailed, the most intelligent practice has resulted. The nineteenth century was suffused with his principles, and his method has become the basis of all subsequent reform. The significance of both his theory and practice has become more and more evident as the years have passed.

The Spread of Pestalozzian Schools and Methods through Europe

Pestalozzi's principles were spread by his disciples throughout Europe, — Switzerland,

The principles of Pestalozzi and institutions similar to his were soon spread by his assistants and others throughout Europe. Strange to say, as a result of their familiarity with his weaknesses and the conservatism resulting from isolation, the Swiss were, as a whole, rather slow to incorporate the Pestalozzian improvements in their school organization and methods of teaching. Zürich was, however, an exception to the general rule. This city was naturally more progressive and had previously been a seat of reform in matters religious.[1] Here Zeller of Würtemberg, who had visited Burgdorf and lectured at Hofwyl, was early invited to give three courses of lectures in aid of the establishment of a teachers' seminary upon the Pestalozzian principles. A large number of teachers, clergymen, and persons of prominence heard these lectures, and thus increased the body of those disseminating the new educational reforms.

[1] See Graves, *A History of Education during the Transition*, pp. 189 f.

Krüsi, after leaving the institute at Yverdun, also founded a number of schools and carried Pestalozzian-ism into various parts of Switzerland. He finally, in 1833, became the director of a teachers' seminary at his native village of Gais. Near this institution he founded two Pestalozzian schools under the management of his daughter, and during the last decade of his life contributed largely to the Pestalozzian literature. Many other disciples eventually started or reorganized schools in various parts of Switzerland upon the principles of Pestalozzi, and, before the middle of the nineteenth century, educational conditions had greatly changed in Switzerland. Pestalozzi's 'observation' methods were in general use, every canton had its 'farm school,' and industrial training had been introduced into most of the normal schools.

But the reforms never secured the hold upon the coun-try of their origin that they did in Germany. The innovations were most remarkable in Prussia, and the system there has, in consequence, often been referred to as the 'Prussian-Pestalozzian.' By the beginning of the nineteenth century Pestalozzianism began to find its way there. In 1801 the appeal of Pestalozzi for a public subscription in behalf of his project at Burgdorf was warmly supported. The next year the publication by Herbart of *Pestalozzi's A B C of Observation* attracted much attention. A representative was sent from

Prussia,

Prussia to Burgdorf to report upon the new system in 1803. Meanwhile the Pestalozzian missionaries were fast converting the land. Plamann, who had visited Burgdorf, established in 1805, after several other educational enterprises, a Pestalozzian school in Berlin,[1] and published several books applying the new methods to language, geography, and natural history. The same year Grüner opened a similar school at Frankfurt, which was later the means of starting Froebel upon an educational career. Zeller was coaxed away from Würtemberg, and in the seminary at Königsberg lectured to large audiences, and organized a Pestalozzian orphanage there. A similar institution for educating orphans was opened at Potsdam by von Türck. In 1808, two of Pestalozzi's pupils, Nicolovius and Süvern, were made directors of public instruction in Prussia, and sent seventeen brilliant young men to Yverdun to study for three years. Upon their return these vigorous youthful educators zealously advanced the cause. The greatest impulse, however, was given the movement by the philosopher, Fichte. In the course of his *Addresses to the German Nation*, 1807–1808, he described the work of Pestalozzi and declared : —

"To the course of instruction which has been invented and brought forward by Heinrich Pestalozzi, and which is now being

[1] Froebel taught in this school while studying at the University of Berlin. See p. 199.

successfully carried out under his direction, must we look for our regeneration." [1]

In this position Fichte was ardently supported by King Friedrich Wilhelm III, and even more by his noble queen, Luise, who now felt that only through these advanced educational principles could a restoration of the territory and prestige lost to Napoleon at Jena be effected. Throughout his reign the king took the keenest interest in the Pestalozzian schools, and the queen frequently went to visit the institutions of Zeller.

A similar spirit was animating the other states of Germany. As early as 1803, Bavaria sent an educator named Müller to Burgdorf to study the methods, and upon his return he started a school at Mainz. Saxony authorized Blochmann, a former pupil of Pestalozzi, to reorganize its schools upon the new basis. Through Denzel, Würtemberg introduced the new methods, and during the first decade of the century many Pestalozzians were appointed seminary directors and school inspectors. Denzel also organized the school system for the duchy of Nassau. The Princess Pauline of Detmold and other rulers were likewise eager to improve the education of their realms by the introduction

and other states of Germany,

[1] The *Reden an die Deutsche Nation* number fourteen in all. This indorsement of Pestalozzi's principles occurs in the tenth.

of the new principles. Everywhere in Germany the greatest enthusiasm prevailed among teachers, state officials, and princes.

Thus in place of the reading, singing, and memorizing of texts, songs, and catechism, under the direction of incompetent choristers and sextons, with unsanitary buildings and brutal punishment, all Germany has come to have in each village an institution for training real men and women. Each school is under the guidance of a devoted, humane, and seminary-bred teacher, and the methods in religion, reading, arithmetic, history, geography, and elementary science are vitalized and interesting. Moreover, the industrial work suggested by Pestalozzi and Fellenberg is in successful operation in most of the reform schools, as well as in the *Fortbildungsschulen* ('continuation schools') of the regular system. As a result, the German schools have for the past three or four generations been considered models, and have been visited by educators and distinguished men from every land.

France,   In France the spread of Pestalozzianism was at first prevented by the military spirit of the time and by the apathy in education, and later, when the reaction occurred, the schools came under ecclesiastical control and had little influence upon the people. Nevertheless, there were evidences of interest in the new doctrines. General Jullien came to Yverdun to study the methods, and issued two commendatory reports, which induced some thirty French pupils to go to Pestalozzi's institute. Chavannes also published a treatise upon the Pestalozzian methods in 1805. Three years later the philosopher, de Biran, founded a Pestalozzian school under the management of a certain Barraud, whom he had sent to study under Pestalozzi. These efforts, however, had little effect upon education, and the Pestalozzian principles did not make much headway in France up to the revolution of 1830. After that time they rapidly became popular, especially through Victor Cousin. This famous professor and minister of public instruction issued in 1835 a *Report on the State of Public Instruction in Prussia*, which showed the great merit of Pestalozzianism in the elementary schools of that country. The other great minister, Guizot, had likewise recommended the Prussian schools as the best type for the reform movement, and had shown himself most zealous in training teachers for their vocation after the ideals of Pestalozzi.

Spain at first took kindly to the new methods. A few schools were founded on these principles, and a number of pupils sent to Pestalozzi through the government, but a reaction soon occurred and education was turned over to the ecclesiastical authorities. In Russia the Czar showed himself interested in Pestalozzi's work, a school similar to the 'institutes' was founded, and a former assistant of Pestalozzi became tutor to the

Spain,

Russia,

royal princes, but probably nothing permanent was accomplished. Schools were also established before long in Italy, Denmark, and Holland by Pestalozzians, but none of them met with much success, and continental Europe in general eventually adopted the new principles indirectly from Germany.

England, and elsewhere.

In England there was a tendency to combine Pestalozzianism with the Bell-Lancaster 'monitorial'[1] system and to adopt rather its formal methodological aspects than its underlying spirit. However, the Pestalozzian school of Dr. Mayo and his sister near London during the second quarter of the century was famous both for its methods and its teachers. The Mayos, together with a friend and admirer of Pestalozzi, named Greaves, and the reformer's biographer, Biber, did much at this time for the cause of educational reform. Through their efforts, with the coöperation of many other educators, 'The Home and Colonial Society'[2] was established in 1836 largely upon Pestalozzian principles, and a number of training schools were founded. The industrial training of Pestalozzi has also found a foothold in England, and in the well-known Red Hill school and farm for young criminals and in other institutions it has produced remarkable results.

[1] See pp. 237–243.
[2] See footnote on p. 229.

Pestalozzianism in the United States

Pestalozzianism began to appear in the United States as early as the first decade of the nineteenth century. It was introduced, not only from the original centers in Switzerland, but indirectly in the form it had assumed in Germany, France, England, and other countries. The instances of its appearance were sporadic and seem to have been but little connected at any time. The earliest presentation was that made from the treatise of Chavannes in 1805 by William McClure. This gentleman was a retired Scotch-American merchant and man of science, who had, upon the invitation of Napoleon, gone to visit the orphanage at Paris directed by Joseph Neef, a former teacher at Burgdorf. Mr. McClure afterward spent much time at the institute in Yverdun, and by his writings, articles, and financial support did much to make the new principles known in the United States. In 1806 he induced Neef to come to America and become his "master's apostle in the new world." Neef maintained an institution at Philadelphia for three years and afterward founded and taught schools in several parts of the country. But his imperfect acquaintance with English and with American character and his frequent migrations prevented his personal influence from being greatly felt, and the two excellent works that he published upon applications

M

In the United States Pestalozzianism was introduced by William McClure through Joseph Neef;

of the Pestalozzian methods were given scant attention.[1]

a large
number of
articles and
translations
were pub-
lished on the
subject; and
applications
were made
by Colburn,
Guyot, and
Mason.

A large variety of literature, describing the new education, and translating the accounts of Chavannes, Jullien, Cousin, and a number of the German educationalists, also appeared in the American educational and other journals during the first half of the century. Returned travelers, like Professor John Griscom, published accounts of their visits and experiences at Yverdun and Hofwyl, and such lecturers as the Rev. Charles Brooks began to suggest the new principles as a remedy for our educational deficiencies. The Pestalozzian methods were applied to arithmetic by Warren Colburn, who spread ' mental arithmetic ' throughout the country, and in his famous *First Lessons* even printed the 'table of units'; to geography by Arnold Guyot, a pupil of Ritter's; to music by Lowell Mason, who was influenced by the works of Nägeli; and to various other subjects ·by a number of educators. Bronson Alcott and his brother urged and practiced the principles of Pestalozzi in their schools, and David P. Page, as principal of the New York State Normal School, utilized the spirit and many of the methods of the Swiss reformer.

The most in-
fluential
movements,
however,

The most influential propaganda of the Pestalozzian doctrines in the United States, however, came through the account of the German school methods in the *Seventh*

[1] For a further account of Neef's work, see *Education*, Vol. XIV, pp. 449–461.

Annual Report (1843) of Horace Mann, and through the inauguration of the 'Oswego methods' by Dr. Edward A. Sheldon. Mann spoke most enthusiastically of the success of the Prussian-Pestalozzian system of education and hinted at the need of a radical reform along the same lines in America. The report caused a great sensation, and was bitterly combated by a group of thirty-one Boston schoolmasters and by conservative sentiment throughout the country. Nevertheless, the suggested reforms were largely effected, and were carried much further by the successors of Mann in the secretaryship of the Massachusetts State Board of Education.[1]

Dr. Sheldon, on the other hand, caught his Pestalozzian inspiration from Toronto, Canada, where he became acquainted with the Mayo methods through publications of the Home and Colonial Society. He resolved to introduce the principles of Pestalozzi into the Oswego schools, of which he was at that time superintendent, and in 1861 sent to the Society in London for an experienced Pestalozzian to train his teachers in these methods. After a year and a half of the experiment, a committee of distinguished educators, who had been invited to inspect the work, pronounced the Oswego movement an unqualified success. Superintendent Sheldon had from the first admitted a few teachers from outside to. learn the new methods, and in 1865 the Oswego training school was made a state institution.

----

[1] See pp. 260 f.

(margin notes) were brought about by Horace Mann's *Seventh Annual Report*

and by Dr. Sheldon's 'Oswego methods.'

Thus was established the first normal school in the United States, where object lessons were the chief feature, and where classes were conducted by model teachers and practice teaching afforded under the supervision of critic teachers. The excellent teachers graduated from this institution caused the Oswego methods to be widely known throughout the country. A large number of other normal schools upon the same basis sprang up rapidly in many states, and the Oswego methods crept into the training schools and the public system of numerous cities. As a consequence, during the third quarter of the nineteenth century, Pestalozzianism had a prevailing influence upon the teachers and courses of the elementary schools in the United States.

Pestalozzi's industrial education was introduced by Woodbridge and Miss Carpenter, and by the institution of special types of colleges and schools.

The industrial phases of Pestalozzi's and Fellenberg's work, however, were slower in coming into the United States than into most of the European countries. They were given publicity through the descriptions of William C. Woodbridge in the *American Journal of Education* and the *American Annals of Education* in 1831–1832, after his visit to Hofwyl, and through articles by others on the subject, and were rapidly introduced into various types of schools. It was not, however, until 1873, with the visit of Miss Mary Carpenter, the English prison reformer, that the 'contract labor' of the reformatories began to be replaced with farming, gardening, and kindred domestic industries. But in the second quarter of the nineteenth century a very large number of institutions of secondary or higher grade with manual labor features, in addition to the literary work, sprang into existence in the United States. The students were thus enabled to obtain exercise and self-support throughout their course. Little attention was given to the pedagogical principles underlying this work, however, and as material conditions improved and formal social life developed, the industrial work of most of these institutions was given up. Further, such schools as Carlisle, Hampton, and Tuskegee adopted industrial training for some special type of education, and the work has also been largely used in the education of defectives. Within the last decade there has been a growing tendency to employ industrial training for the sake of holding pupils longer in school and increasing the efficiency of the public system. In so far as this has tended to replace the more general educational values of manual training, once so popular, with skill in some special industrial process, this modern movement represents a return to Pestalozzi.

SUPPLEMENTARY READING [1]

I. Sources

NEEF, F. J. N. *Sketch of a Plan and Method of Education* and *The Method of Instructing Children Rationally in the Arts of Reading and Writing.*

[1] For a more complete bibliography of Pestalozzian literature, see Barnard, *Pestalozzi and his Educational System*, pp. 167–184.

*PESTALOZZI, J. H.   *The Evening Hour of a Hermit, Letters on Early Education,*[1] *Leonard and Gertrude,* and *How Gertrude Teaches Her Children.*

II. AUTHORITIES

BACHMAN, F. P.   *The Social Factor in Pestalozzi's Theory of Education* (*Education,* Vol. XXII, pp. 402–414).

*GUIMPS, R. DE.   *Pestalozzi, His Aim and Work.* (Translated by Crombie.)

HAMILTON, C. J.   *Henri Pestalozzi* (*Educational Review,* Vol. III, pp. 173–184).

HÈRISSON, F.   *Pestalozzi, élève de J. J. Rousseau.*

*HOLMAN, H.   *Pestalozzi.*

HOYT, C. O.   *Studies in the History of Modern Education.*   Chap. III.

KELLOGG, A. M.   *Life of Pestalozzi.*

*KRÜSI, H.   *Pestalozzi, His Life, Work, and Influence.*

MISAWA, T.   *Modern Educators and Their Ideals.*   Chap. VI.

MONROE, W. S.   *Joseph Neef and Pestalozzianism in the United States* (*Education,* Vol. XIV, pp. 449–461).

MORF, H.   *Zur Biographie Pestalozzi's.*

MUNROE, J. P.   *The Educational Ideal.*   Pp. 179–187.

PAYNE, J.   *Lectures on the History of Education.*   Lect. IX.

*PINLOCHE, A.   *Pestalozzi and the Foundation of the Modern Elementary School.*

*QUICK, R. H.   *Educational Reformers.*   Pp. 354–383.

SHELDON, E. A.   *The Oswego Movement.*

[1] A series of letters written in 1818–1820 to J. P. Greaves, an Englishman who had taught at Yverdun for a time and then returned home.

CHAPTER X

HERBART AND EDUCATION AS A SCIENCE

A MOST elaborate development of Pestalozzi's principles was that introduced by Herbart. This great educationalist was first inspired by the Swiss reformer, but his careful training and his keen philosophical insight caused him to work out more clearly and definitely the 'observation' and the pedagogical devices of his homely master until they formed a well-rounded system. He stressed the educational process from the standpoint of the teacher, and paid the most minute attention to method. He is the first example of the philosopher and psychologist in education. His contemporary, Froebel, was an immediate pupil and colleague of Pestalozzi, and probably owed more to his influence. He, however, lacked the complete philosophic insight and training of Herbart, and never became quite as clear and systematic, or paid such minute attention to method.

Herbart developed Pestalozzi's principles elaborately, emphasizing the teacher and method.

The Early Career and Writings of Herbart

Johann Friedrich Herbart (1776–1841) both by birth and education possessed a remarkable mind and was well calculated to become a profound educational philosopher. All his traditions were intellectual. His

Herbart's traditions were all intellectual, and while still in the

gymnasium
and univer-
sity he
greatly
distinguished
himself.

paternal grandfather was rector of the gymnasium at
Oldenburg, Herbart's native town, and his father was
a lawyer and privy councilor there. Moreover, the
mother of Herbart is known to have been 'a rare and
wonderful woman,' who was able to assist her son in
his Greek and mathematics, and to do much toward
directing his education. While still a youth in the
gymnasium, Herbart showed that he himself possessed
that 'many-sided and balanced interest' he afterward
commended, and soon distinguished himself by writing
essays upon moral freedom and other metaphysical
subjects. At the University of Jena, under the inspiration of Fichte, he produced incisive critiques upon the
treatises of that philosopher and of the other great
idealist of the age, Schelling, and began to work out his
own system of thought. Just before graduation, how-

As a private
tutor he ob-
tained his
only practical
experience in
pedagogy.

ever, Herbart left the university to become private tutor
to the three sons of Herr von Steiger-Reggisberg, Governor of Interlaken, Switzerland. During the two years
(1797–1799) that he occupied this position, he obtained
his only real practical experience in pedagogy. He was
required by his patron to make bi-monthly a written report of the methods he used and of his pupils' progress
in their studies and conduct. Five of these letters are
still extant, and reveal the germs of the elaborate system
that was afterward to bear the name of Herbart. The
youthful pedagogue seems thus early to have based his

methods of training upon psychology. He showed a due regard for the respective ages and individualities of his pupils, and undertook to develop in them the elements of morality and a 'many-sided interest.'

While in Switzerland, Herbart met Pestalozzi and was greatly attracted by the underlying principles of that reformer. He paid a visit to the institute at Burgdorf in 1799, and during the next two years, while at Bremen completing his interrupted university course, he attempted to render more scientific the thought of the Swiss educator. It was at this time that Herbart wrote a critical, but kindly, essay *On Pestalozzi's Latest Writing, 'How Gertrude Teaches Her Children,'* [1] and made his interpretation of *Pestalozzi's Idea of an A B C of Observation.* [2] In the former work, Herbart gives an account of the aim and methods of Pestalozzi and shows the development of his own ideas from Pestalozzianism. The latter treatise describes the value, cultivation, and use of observation, and attempts to found the method of Pestalozzi upon a definite mathematical theory.

Having met Pestalozzi at Burgdorf, he undertook to interpret that reformer's principles in two essays.

His *Moral Revelation of the World* and His *General Pedagogy*

Following this period, from 1802 to 1809, Herbart lectured [3] on pedagogy at the University of Göttingen.

While lecturing at Göttingen, Herbart

[1] *Ueber Pestalozzi's neueste Schrift: Wie Gertrud ihre Kinder lehrte.*
[2] *Pestalozzi's Idee eines A B C der Anschauung.*
[3] His position was at first that of a *Privatdocent.* See p. 68, footnote 2.

further interpreted Pestalozzi, and wrote his own *Moral Revelation of the World* and his work on *General Pedagogy.*

While here, among other pedagogical works, he formulated his final position *On the Point of View in Judging the Pestalozzian Method of Instruction*,[1] and published his ideas *On the Moral Revelation of the World as the Chief Function of Education.*[2] By this time he seems to have largely crystallized his own system. Pestalozzi had by his later works made evident the faults in his methods, and Herbart no longer strives to conceal their vagueness and want of system. In both of the Göttingen treatises he further insists upon 'educative instruction,' or real ethical training. Sense perception, he holds with Pestalozzi, does supply the first elements of knowledge, but the material of the school course should be arranged with reference to the general purpose of instruction, which is moral self-realization.[2] His position was made even clearer in his standard work on *General Pedagogy*,[3] which he produced shortly afterward.

---

[1] *Ueber den Standpunkt der Beurtheilung der Pestalozzischen Unterrichtsmethode.*

[2] *Ueber die ästhetische Darstellung der Welt als Hauptgeschäft der Erziehung.* With Herbart, ethics is the main branch of 'æsthetics,' and deals with such relations among volitions as please or displease. This work was originally intended as an appendix to the second edition of his *Pestalozzi's Idea of an A B C of Sense Observation*, but it proved to be a forerunner of his *General Pedagogy*. It contains in outline all the positions systematically developed in the more elaborate treatise.

[3] *Allgemeine Pädagogik.*

His Seminary and Practice School at Königsberg

In 1809 Herbart was called to the chair of philosophy at Königsberg as practically the successor of the illustrious Immanuel Kant,[1] and there did his great work for educational theory and practice. He soon established his now historic pedagogical seminary and the practice school connected with it. This constituted the first attempt at experimentation and a scientific study of education on the basis now generally employed in universities. The students, who taught in the practice school under the supervision and criticism of the professor, were intending to become school principals and inspectors, and, through the widespread work and influence of these young Herbartians, the educational system of Prussia and of every other state in Germany was greatly advanced. In his numerous publications at Königsberg, Herbart devoted himself chiefly to developing a series of works on his system of psychology, but he also wrote a number of essays and letters upon education. The conservatism and opposition to free inquiry in Prussia, however, eventually became too restrictive for a man of Herbart's progressive temperament.

As Kant's successor at Königsberg, he established his famous pedagogical seminary and practice school, and wrote chiefly on psychology.

[1] Kant died in 1804, and was succeeded by Wilhelm Traugott Krug, who resigned in 1809 to accept the chair at Leipzig.

The Matured System in His *Outlines*

Late in life, he returned to Göttingen, and published his *Outlines of Pedagogical Lectures* and his *Outlines of General Pedagogy.*

After serving nearly a quarter of a century in Königsberg, he accepted a call to a professorship at Göttingen, and the last eight years of his life were spent in expanding his pedagogical positions and lecturing with great approval at his old station. Here, in 1835, he published his *Outlines of Pedagogical Lectures,*[1] in which six years later he embodied his *Outlines of General Pedagogy.*[2] This treatise gives an exposition of his educational system when fully matured, together with its relation to psychology. The work proved to be his swan's song, for, shortly after the new edition appeared, Herbart died at the height of his reputation.[3]

Herbart's 'Ideas' and 'Apperception Masses'

Some knowledge of Herbart's psychology is necessary, in order to understand his educational principles.

To understand the educational principles of Herbart, it is necessary to know something of his psychology and of the metaphysics lying back of it. With the possible exception of Kant's educational theories, Herbart's was the first real system of education that was

---

[1] *Umriss pädagogischer Vorlesungen.*

[2] *Umriss der allgemeinen Pädagogik.*

[3] His complete works were not published until 1850, when Hartenstein collected them. The most satisfactory collection at present is that found in the seventh edition of Bartholomäi, revised by von Sallwürk (Langensalza, 1903).

based upon a psychology worked out by the founder. His psychological positions have now been almost entirely abandoned or reconstructed, but the idea of founding education upon psychology has been productive of a marked advance in educational theory. This system of psychology was an outgrowth of his own introspection. With Herbart, the simplest elements of consciousness are 'ideas,' which result from the varying states into which the soul is thrown in endeavoring to maintain itself against external stimuli. Once produced, the ideas become existences with their own dynamic force, and constantly strive to preserve themselves.[1] They struggle to attain as nearly as possible to the summit of consciousness, and each idea tends to draw into consciousness or heighten those allied to it, and to depress or force out those which are unlike. Hence in the constant interaction between ideas present

[1] This psychology is part of a pluralistic metaphysics somewhat resembling the doctrine of 'ideas' in Plato or Kant's 'Dinge an sich,' and even more the 'monadology' of Leibnitz. Herbart assumes an unseen universe, composed of 'units' called 'reals,' which are unchangeable and constitute the 'noumena' of which our experiences are the 'phenomena.' His 'reals,' however, are mere existences, and, unlike the 'monads,' do not possess activity of any sort, save that of 'self-preservation' against annihilation. The soul is simply a species of superior 'real.' Its sole function in psychology seems to be that of producing the ideas or mind atoms in reaction to the outside world, for once the ideas are born they go on by their own laws, and the parent 'soul' plays no further part in their life.

'Similar' ideas fuse, 'disparate' ideas combine, and 'contrary' ideas repel;

at the same time in consciousness, 'similar' ideas fuse or combine into a homogeneous whole, and become more powerful in resisting all efforts to drive them out of consciousness; 'disparate' ideas, or those which cannot be compared, also combine, but form a complex or group rather than an indistinguishable unity; while 'contrary,' or hostile ideas, produce actual opposition, and each attempts to drive the other out of consciousness. For example, 'sweetness' and 'whiteness' would be 'disparate' ideas, since they are not of the same class and might coexist in our idea of an object, but 'whiteness' and 'blackness' are so 'contrary' that one would necessarily contradict the other. Each new idea or group of ideas is, therefore, retained, modified, or rejected according to its degree of harmony or conflict with the previously existing ideas.[1] In other words, all new ideas are interpreted through those already in consciousness. This principle,

hence we have 'apperception,' or the interpretation of all new ideas through

which Herbart called *apperception*, is the central doctrine in his whole educational system, and he constantly returns to it from many different angles. In accordance with 'apperception' the teacher can hope to

[1] Herbart here develops a complete mechanics of ideas. On the analogy of psychical tensions to physical forces, he works out a system of mental statics and dynamics that may be quantitatively determined. Mental action and reaction are set forth in mathematical equations; the involution and evolution of thought are expressed numerically, and ideas are arranged in a series.

secure interest and the attention of the pupil to any those already in conscious- ness. new idea or set of ideas and have him retain it, only through making use of his body of related knowledge. The educational problem thus becomes how to present new material in such a way that it can be 'apperceived,' or incorporated with the old. Hence, too, the soul of the pupil is largely in the hands of the teacher, since he can make or modify his 'apperception masses,' or systems of ideas.

The Moral and Religious Aim of Education

It is probably because of this control of the pupil's The aim of education is attainment of character. destiny by his instructors that Herbart holds the aim of education should be to establish the moral life or character. His *Outlines* opens with the statement: —

"The term 'virtue' expresses the whole purpose of education. Virtue is the idea of 'inner freedom,' which has developed into an abiding actuality in an individual. Whence, as inner freedom is a relation between 'insight' and 'volition,' a double task is at once set before the teacher. It becomes his business to make actual each one of these factors separately, in order that later a permanent relationship may result."

In other words, virtue is attained by the pupil when Besides 'inner free- dom,' or the harmoniza- tion of con- duct with 'insight,' Herbart his perception of what is right and wrong is in com- plete accord with his deeds, and the aim of education should, therefore, be to instil such ideas as will develop both his understanding of the moral order and a con-

formulates the moral concepts of 'efficiency of will,' 'good will,' 'justice,' and 'equity.'

scientious spirit in carrying it out. "To induce the pupil to make this effort," Herbart admits, "is a difficult achievement. It is easy enough, by the study of the example of others, to cultivate theoretical acumen; the moral application to the pupil himself, however, can be successfully made only in so far as his inclinations and habits have taken a direction in keeping with his insight." To make clearer the meaning of this 'inner freedom' and the ethical aim, Herbart formulates four subsidiary moral concepts, which make up the elements of character and must be understood by the teacher. These are 'efficiency of will,' which includes positiveness of purpose, vigor in action, and harmony with the ethical order of the world; 'good will,' or recognition of the welfare of others as if it were one's own; 'justice,' the idea of rights, which demands abstinence from contention; and 'equity,' which arises when existing relations are changed for good or evil, and is the basis of society's systems of punishments or rewards. These five fundamental concepts should from the first be incorporated into the pupil's stock of ideas.

Morality and religion are both needed.

But even the attainment of moral living is not sufficient. Herbart declares:—

"It is necessary to combine moral education proper, which in everyday life lays stress continually on correct self-determination, with religious training. The notion that something really worthy has been achieved, needs to be tempered by humility. Conversely, religious education has need of the moral also to forestall cant and hypocrisy, which are only too apt to appear where morality has not already secured a firm foothold through earnest self-questioning and self-criticism with a view to improvement."

'Many-Sided Interest' and the 'Historical' and 'Scientific' Studies

The making of the *morally religious man* is, therefore, Herbart's idea of the end of education. His ultimate aim must, however, be attained through instruction, and since that medium has to deal with the human mind, the more immediate purpose must be based upon psychology, just as the final goal is dependent upon ethics. It is obvious to Herbart that existing instruction has not succeeded, because it is based upon a false psychological theory. He maintains that "what is customarily ascribed to the action of the various 'faculties' takes place in certain groups of ideas." [1] Even 'will,' upon which man's character rests, is not to be regarded as an 'independent faculty.' "Volition has its root in thought," he claims, "not, indeed, in the details one knows, but certainly in the combination and

[1] From the nature of Herbart's psychology, the soul or self cannot, as with Leibnitz or Kant, be an original synthetic activity, which forms experience. It cannot be possessed of innate powers or 'faculties,' as supposed by those who would treat the chief types of mental states as real forces, but consists merely of the aggregate of ideas and their combinations.

N

To produce the 'morally religious man,' a study must be made of his thought systems, and such studies as will appeal to them and furnish a 'moral revelation of the world ' must be given him.

total effect of the acquired ideas." A careful study must, accordingly, be made of each pupil's thought masses, temperament, and mental capacity and processes, to determine how instruction may furnish a 'moral revelation of the world.' In Herbart's judgment: —

"Instruction in the sense of mere information-giving contains no guarantee whatever that it will materially counteract faults and influence existing groups of ideas that are independent of the imparted information. But it is these ideas that education must reach; for the kind and extent of assistance that instruction may render to conduct may depend upon the hold it has upon them."

There is not much likelihood of the pupil's receiving ideas of virtue that will develop into glowing ideals of conduct when his studies do not appeal to his thought systems and are consequently regarded with indifference and aversion. They must coalesce with the ideas he already has, and thus touch his life, if interest is to be felt and will aroused. Instruction must be so selected and arranged as to appeal to the previous experience of the pupil, and to reveal all the relations of life and conduct in their fullness. To expand the mental horizon and open every avenue of approach to his ideas, interests, and will, it is necessary that the pupil should be given as broad instruction as possible. In this way only can a wide range of ideas be furnished and the necessary 'many-sided interest' created. In analyzing the 'many-sided interest,' Herbart further holds that ideas and interests spring from two main sources, — 'experience,' which furnishes us with a knowledge of nature, and 'social intercourse,' from which come the sentiments toward our fellow men. Interests may, therefore, be classed as belonging to (1) 'knowledge' or (2) 'participation.' These two sets of interests, in turn, Herbart divides into three groups each. He classes the 'knowledge' interests as (a) 'empirical,' appealing directly to the senses; (b) 'speculative,' seeking to perceive the relations of cause and effect; and (c) 'æsthetic,' resting upon the enjoyment of contemplation. The 'participation' interests are divided into (a) 'sympathetic,' dealing with relations to other individuals; (b) 'social,' including the community as a whole; and (c) 'religious,' treating one's relations to the Divine. After making this analysis of the six types of interest that are needed, he also dilates upon the dangers of one-sidedness in each case, and endeavors to "bring out more clearly the manifold phases of interest that must be taken into account."

For Herbart, then, just as religious morality is the final aim of education, the more immediate purpose of instruction is *many-sided interest*. "Instruction," he declares, "will form the circle of thought, and education the character. The last is nothing without the first. Herein is contained the whole sum of my pedagogy." Since character is thus to develop through the medium of instruction and the growth of concrete knowledge, which

There is needed a 'many-sided interest.'

This will include interests of (1) 'knowledge,' which are divided into 'empirical,' 'speculative,' and 'æsthetic,' and of (2) 'participation,' which are divided into 'sympathetic,' 'social,' and 'religious.'

should be as broad as possible, the subject-matter of the curriculum should cover the entire range of known ideas. Hence, to correspond to the two main groups of interests, Herbart divides all studies into two main branches, — the (1) 'historical,' including history, literature, and languages; and the (2) 'scientific,' embracing mathematics and industrial training, as well as the natural sciences. But, while all these subjects are needed for a 'many-sided interest' and the various studies have for convenience been separated and classified by themselves, they must be so arranged in the curriculum as to become unified and an organic whole, if the unity of the pupil's consciousness is to be maintained. Concerning this Herbart holds : —

Corresponding to the two groups of interests, studies are divided into (1) 'historical,' including history, literature, and languages, and (2) 'scientific,' embracing sciences, mathematics, and industrial training.

"‚Scattering no less than one-sidedness forms an antithesis to many-sidedness. Many-sidedness is to be the basis of virtue ; but the latter is an attribute of personality, hence it is evident that the unity of self-consciousness must not be impaired. The business of instruction is to form the person on many sides, and accordingly to avoid a distracting or dissipating effect. And instruction has successfully avoided this in the case of one who with ease surveys his well-arranged knowledge *in all of its unifying relations* and beholds it together as *his very own*."

But while many-sidedness is desirable, all studies must be unified and scattering avoided.

'Correlation,' 'Concentration,' and the 'Culture Epochs'

This position of Herbart forecasts the emphasis upon *correlation*, or the unification of studies, so common among his followers. The principle was further developed by later Herbartians under the name of *concen-*

Hence the Herbartians later formulated 'correlation' and 'concentra-

tration, or the unifying of all subjects about one common central study, such as literature or history. But the selection and articulation of the subject-matter in such a way as to arouse many-sidedness and harmony is not more than hinted at by Herbart himself. He specifically holds, however, that Homer's *Odyssey* should be the first work read, since this represents the interests and activities of the race while in its youth, and would appeal to the individual during the same stage. He would follow this epic with the *Iliad*, the *Philoctetes* of Sophocles, the histories of Xenophon, Plato's dialogues, and other classics, in the order of the growing complexity of racial interests depicted in them.[1] This tentative endeavor of Herbart, in the selection of material for the course of study, to parallel the development of the individual with that of the race, was also continued and enlarged by the disciples of Herbart. It especially became definite and fixed in the *culture epoch theory* formulated by Ziller and others.[2]

tion,' and the 'culture epoch theory.'

'Absorption and Reflection' and the 'Formal Steps of Instruction'

But to secure this broad range of material and to unify and systematize it, Herbart realized that it was necessary

[1] Herbart's attitude on the development of interests in the race is most fully brought out in his *General Pedagogy*, Introduction and Chapter V, I (see Felkin's translation, *Science of Education*, pp. 91 and 164 ff.).

[2] See p. 188.

In the educational process Herbart distinguished between 'absorption,' the acquisition of facts, and 'reflection,' the assimilation of knowledge thus gained;
to formulate a method of instructing the child. Due sequence and order must be introduced to shape the material into a well-arranged structure. This plan of instruction he wished to conform to the development and working of the human mind, and in this connection introduced his distinction between *absorption and reflection*.[1] This twofold mental process is necessary in grasping all new knowledge, and the alternation between the two steps has sometimes been described as the 'breathing' of the mind. 'Absorption' is giving oneself up to acquisition or contemplation of facts or ideas, and 'reflection' is the unification or assimilation of the manifold knowledge gained by absorption. As these two stages are mutually exclusive, the pupil passes in psychical development from one to the other. On the basis of this description of mental activity and growth, Herbart worked out the outlines of his logical method in instruction, which he states as follows: —

"We prescribe the general rule: give equal prominence to absorption and reflection in every group of objects, even the smallest; that is to say, emphasize equally clearness of the individual perception, association of the manifold, coördination of the associated, and progress through exercise according to this coördination."

and formulated the four steps in his
Of the four steps indicated in this method, (1) *clearness*, the presentation of facts or elements to be learned,

[1] See *Outlines*, § 66, and *General Pedagogy*, Bk. II, Chap. I, § 1.

is purely 'absorption'; (2) *association*, the uniting of these with related facts previously acquired, is mainly 'absorption,' but contains elements of 'reflection'; (3) *system*, the coherent and logical arrangement of what has been associated, is non-progressive or passive 'reflection'; and (4) *method*, the practical application of the system by the pupil to new data, is progressive or active 'reflection.' The formulation of this method was made only in principle by Herbart, but it has since been largely modified and developed by his followers. It was soon felt that, on the principle of 'apperception,' the pupil must first be made conscious of his existing stock of ideas so far as they are similar to the material to be presented, and that this can be accomplished by a review of preceding lessons or by an outline of what is to be undertaken, or by both procedures. Hence Herbart's noted disciple, Ziller, divided the step of 'clearness' into *preparation* and *presentation*, and the more recent Herbartian, Rein, added *aim* as a substep to 'preparation.' The names of the other three processes have been changed for the sake of greater lucidity and significance by the later Herbartians, and the five *formal* (*i.e.* 'rational') *steps of instruction* [1] are now generally given as (1) *preparation*, (2) *presentation*, (3) *comparison* and *abstraction*, (4) *generalization*, and (5) *application*.[2] Herbart also made numer-

method of instruction, — 'clearness,' 'association,' 'system,' and 'method,' which have been expanded and modified by the Herbartians.

[1] *Die formalen Stufen des Unterrichts.*
[2] Cf. McMurry's *Method of the Recitation.*

ous other suggestive analyses and interpretations of the mechanics of instruction.[1]

'Government' and 'Training' in Discipline

In discipline Herbart makes repressive 'government' a preliminary to 'training' or real moral education.

As a corollary of his improvements in method, Herbart's ideas concerning discipline are important and well worthy of consideration. While he admits the need of 'government,' which is repressive, he sharply distinguishes this from 'training,' or real moral education, for which the former is intended to prepare. The purpose of government is to hold the pupils in order and subservient to the will of the teacher until moral habits are formed. It should keep them properly occupied and supervised, and should issue prohibitions and commands, rewards and punishments. But an irreparable moral injury is wrought if pupils are forever governed and never trained. "The function of training," says Herbart, "does not consist in always restraining and meddling; still less, in grafting the practices of others to take the place of the pupil's self-activity." Training shapes the will for self-control, as cannot be done by constant repression or emotional appeals. Aid and sympathy from the teacher are correlated with confidence and dependence upon the part of the pupil. Training is thus the parent of voluntary coöperation, and should be the ultimate

[1] Such, for example, as his discussion of the educational process under three phases, — *presentative, analytic,* and *synthetic.*

aim of schoolroom discipline. It unites with 'educative instruction' to form character.

The Value and Influence of Herbart's Principles

On all sides, then, as compared with Pestalozzi, Herbart was most logical and comprehensive. The former was primarily a philanthropist and reformer; the latter a psychologist and philosopher. Pestalozzi succeeded in arousing Europe to the need of universal education and of vitalizing the prevailing formalism in the schools, but he was unable with his vague and unsystematic utterances to give guidance and efficiency to the reform forces he had initiated. While he felt the need of 'psychologizing instruction' and of beginning with sense perception for the sake of clear ideas, he had neither the time nor the training to construct a psychology beyond the traditional one of the times, nor to analyze the way the material gained by observation could be assimilated. Herbart, on the other hand, did create a system of psychology that had an immediate bearing upon education. He showed how the product of observation was assimilated through 'apperception,' and maintained the possibility of making all material tend toward moral development through 'educative instruction.' This, he held, could be accomplished by use of the proper courses and methods. In determining the subjects to be selected and articulated, he considered Pestalozzi's emphasis upon the

Herbart clarified the 'psychologizing instruction' and the beginning with sense perception of Pestalozzi, through an original system of psychology and the principle of 'apperception,' and made all tend toward moral development.

He made Pestalozzi's emphasis upon the physical world a stepping-stone, and

stressed history, languages, and literature, rather than arithmetic and the natural sciences.

study of the physical world to be merely a stepping-stone to his own 'moral revelation of the world,' and, while the former made arithmetic, geography, and natural sciences his chief care, he preferred to stress history, languages, and literature. He also first undertook a careful analysis of the successive steps in all instruction.

On the other hand, a great drawback to the Herbartian doctrines is found in their formalization. But while Herbart's psychological system is most mechanical and applies better to the process of instruction than to the human being in general, it has started all the fruitful

While Herbart's principles have tended toward formalization, they have stimulated most fruitful work in psychology and education.

research in psycho-physics, and has worked well as a basis for educational theory and practice. There has been considerable danger, too, that the attempt of Herbart to bring about due sequence and arrangement in instruction would become perverted through his disciples into an inflexible *schema*, but it has, upon the whole, done much to introduce system and order into the work of the classroom. As we shall see, where Froebel undertook to explain Pestalozzi's rather vague conceptions of following the nature of the child by elaborating it on the volitional side, Herbart renders it more explicit by an intellectual interpretation.[1] While Froebel's empha-

---

[1] Similarly, the brainy priest, *Antonio Rosmini-Serbati* (1797–1855), in *The Ruling Principle of Method*, while combining Froebel's development with the 'apperception' of Herbart, strives primarily to interpret Pestalozzi from the emotional standpoint.

sis was upon the child and self-activity, Herbart magnified instruction and the teacher. Therein rest both his strength and weakness and in these formulations of his is indicated how differently from the mystic founder of the kindergarten he had developed the naïve practice and formulations of Pestalozzi.

The Extension of His Doctrines through Disciples in Germany

The theoretical foundations of Herbart, however, were laid mostly in outline. He himself had but little experience in teaching and had no opportunity to work out his principles in the schoolroom. His early disciples, however, were able to fill in and extend his work. They reduced his theories to practice and applied them to the content and methods of the elementary and secondary systems of Germany. From practically the beginning there were two contemporary schools of Herbartianism. In its application of Herbart's theory, the school of Stoy for the most part held closely to the original form; but that headed by Ziller gave it a freer interpretation, and contributed some important modifications and elaborations. Karl Volkmar Stoy had been a student under Herbart after that philosopher's return to Göttingen. He became a professor at Jena, and established there a pedagogical seminary and practice school upon the Herbartian basis. His *Encyclopaedia of Pedagogics* and

His work was extended by his disciples, —

Stoy, who held to the original literally, and Ziller, who interpreted more freely and elaborated;

numerous other educational works were mainly a forceful restatement of Herbart's positions. Tuiskon Ziller, both as a teacher in a gymnasium and as professor at Leipzig, did much to popularize and develop the Herbartian system. His great work, *The Basis of the Doctrine of Educative Instruction*,[1] brought Herbartianism into prominence, and resulted in the formation of the society known as the 'Association for the Scientific Study of Education,'[2] which has since spread throughout Germany. Ziller further emphasized Herbart's division of the curriculum into two groups of studies, and made clear the subordination of the 'scientific' studies to the 'historical.' He also elaborated the doctrines of 'correlation' and 'concentration,' and was the first definitely to formulate the 'culture epoch' theory. "Every pupil should," said he, "pass successively through each of the chief epochs of the general mental development of mankind suitable to his stage of development. The material of instruction, therefore, should be drawn from the thought material of that stage of historical development in culture, which runs parallel with the present mental stage of the pupil."[3] These principles Ziller worked out practically in a course of study for the eight

---

[1] *Grundlegung zur Lehre vom erziehenden Unterricht.*

[2] *Verein für Wissenschaftliche Pädagogik.*

[3] See Felkin's *Introduction to Herbart's Science and Practice of Education*, p. 122.

years of the elementary school, which he centered around fairy tales, Robinson Crusoe, and selections from the Old and New Testaments. He, moreover, developed Herbart's 'formal stages of instruction' by dividing the first step and changing the name of the last.

Other Germans to influence Herbartianism have been Lange, Rein, and Frick. Karl Lange's *Apperception* is an excellent combination of scientific insight and popular presentation. It treats the various problems of education on the basis that "all learning is apperceiving." He agrees in general with the Herbartian method, but warns against its mechanics and formalism. Wilhelm Rein, a pupil of both Stoy and Ziller, succeeded the former at Jena, but is closer to the latter in his interpretation of Herbart. His *Outlines of Pedagogy* [1] shows the development that has taken place since the time of Herbart. He adopts Ziller's 'concentration' and 'culture epochs,' but makes these theories more rational by coördinating other material with the 'historical' center in the curriculum. Otto Frick, director of the 'Francke Institutions' at Halle,[2] inclining more to the literal interpretation of Stoy, devoted himself to applying Herbartianism to the secondary schools.[3] A throng of other German school-

Lange, who reduced all learning to 'apperception';

Rein, who showed the later development of Herbartianism;

Frick, who applied Herbartianism to the secondary schools;

[1] *Pädagogik im Grundriss.*

[2] See pp. 68 ff.

[3] An organic course for *Gymnasien* is outlined in the eighth number of the *Quarterly Magazine*, which he edited.

and many others.

masters and professors have further adapted the doctrines of Herbart to the school, and while their theories differ very largely from one another, from their common basis they are all properly designated 'Herbartian.'

Herbartianism in the United States

In the United States the 'National Herbart Society' has extended Herbart's principles by translating his works and publishing a Year Book.

Next to the land of its birth, the United States has been more influenced by Herbartianism than any other country. The movement was fostered largely by American teachers who had taken the doctor's degree in Germany, and during the last decade of the nineteenth century it attained almost to the proportions of a cult. In 1892 'The National Herbart Society' was founded to extend the scope of these principles and to adapt them to American conditions. The association started immediately to translate the works of Herbart and various German Herbartians, and since 1895 it has regularly published a *Year Book*. Besides these efforts, individual members of the organization have been active in discussing Herbartian principles and their embodiment in our methods of instruction. Charles DeGarmo, professor of Education at Cornell University, who was the first president of the Herbart Society and the editor of its publications, has given wide popularity to many of the principles and has utilized them as the basis of his textbooks. Frank M. McMurry of the Columbia University Teachers College, and his brother, Charles

De Garmo and the McMurrys have also as individuals sought to popularize his principles,

A. McMurry, of the Illinois State Normal University, both by books and articles, have done yeoman service for Herbartianism.

Moreover, many who would hardly consider themselves Herbartians have undertaken to modify and adapt these principles, especially 'correlation' and 'concentration.' Francis W. Parker of Chicago, for example, sought to center the course of study around a hierarchy of natural and social sciences, and his associate, Wilbur S. Jackman, attempted a correlation of science and history. The Committee of Fifteen, appointed by the National Education Association to report upon elementary education, show Herbartian influence in their discussions of 'correlation,' although they give the term a wider interpretation. Various other types of unification about a core of literature, history, or nature study, or, through combination with Froebelianism, of social activities, have been suggested. *while many not Herbartians have used 'correlation' and 'concentration' in modified forms.*

While in this way all elementary and to some extent secondary schools have been affected, Herbartianism in its purity has been largely abandoned for less dogmatic methods. Even the Herbart Society has ceased to exist as a propaganda and has since 1901 been known as 'The National Society for the Scientific Study of Education.' Yet probably no system of pedagogy has had so wide an influence upon American education and upon the thought and practice of teachers generally. *Yet Herbartianism, while most influential, has become less of a propaganda.*

SUPPLEMENTARY READING

I. SOURCES

BARTHOLOMÄI, F.   *Johann Friedrich Herbarts Pädagogische Schriften.*   (Revised by E. von Sallwürk.)

ECKOFF, W. J.   *Herbart's A B C of Sense Perception and Minor Pedagogical Works.*

FELKIN, H. M. and E.   *Herbart's Letters and Lectures on Education.*

*FELKIN, H. M. and E.   *Herbart's Science of Education.*

*LANGE, A. F., and DE GARMO, C.   *Herbart's Outlines of Pedagogical Doctrine.*

*LANGE, K.   *Apperception.*   (Translated by Herbart Club.)

MULLINER, B. C.   *Herbart's Application of Psychology to the Science of Education.*

SMITH, M. K.   *Herbart's Text-book in Psychology.*

VAN LIEW, C. C. and I. J.   *Rein's Outlines of Pedagogics.*

WIGET, T.   *Die Formalen Stufen des Unterrichts.*

II. AUTHORITIES

*ADAMS, J.   *The Herbartian Psychology Applied to Education.*   Chap. III.

COLE, P. R.   *Herbart and Froebel: an Attempt at Synthesis.*

DARROCH, A.   *Herbart and the Herbartian Theory of Education.*   Lect. V.

DE GARMO, C.   *Essentials of Method.*

*DE GARMO, C.   *German Contributions to the Coördination of Studies* (*Educational Review*, Vol. IV, pp. 422–437) and *A Working Basis for the Correlation of Studies* (*Educational Review*, Vol. V, pp. 451–466).

*DE GARMO, C.   *Herbart and the Herbartians.*

FELKIN, H. M. and E.   *An Introduction to Herbart's Science and Practice of Education.*

GILBERT, C. B. *Practicable Correlations of Studies* (*Educational Review*, Vol. XI, pp. 313–322).

*HARRIS, W. T. *Herbart and Pestalozzi Compared* (*Educational Review*, Vol. V, pp. 417–423); *Herbart's Doctrine of Interest* (*Educational Review*, Vol. X, pp. 71–81).

HARRIS, W. T. *The Psychological Foundations of Education.* Chap. XXXVI.

*HERBART SOCIETY. *Year Book.* Nos. I and II.

HUGHES, J. L. *The Educational Theories of Froebel and Herbart* (*Educational Review*, Vol. X, pp. 239–247).

JACKMAN, W. S. *The Correlation of Science and History* (*Educational Review*, Vol. IX, pp. 464–471).

*LUKENS, H. T. *The Correlation of Studies* (*Educational Review*, Vol. X, pp. 364–383).

McMURRY, C. A. *The Elements of General Method.*

McMURRY, F. M. *Concentration* (*Educational Review*, Vol. IX, pp. 27–37).

MACVANNEL, J. A. *The Educational Theories of Herbart and Froebel.*

PARKER, F. W. *Talks on Pedagogics. An Outline of the Theory of Concentration.*

REIN, W. *Pestalozzi and Herbart* (*The Forum*, Vol. XXI, pp. 346–360).

SMITH, M. K. *Herbart's Life* (*New England Journal of Education*, Vol. XXIX, pp. 139 ff.).

TOMPKINS, A. *Herbart's Philosophy and His Educational Theory* (*Educational Review*, Vol. XVI, pp. 233–243).

*UFER, C. *Introduction to the Pedagogy of Herbart.* (Translated by J. C. Zinser.)

VANDEWALKER, N. C. *The Culture Epoch Theory* (*Educational Review*, Vol. XV, pp. 374–391).

VAN LIEW, C. C. *Life of Herbart and Development of his Pedagogical Doctrine.*

WARD, J. *Herbart* (*Encyclopædia Britannica*).

o

CHAPTER XI

FROEBEL AND THE KINDERGARTEN

Froebel developed the principles of Pesta- lozzi along different lines from Herbart. ANOTHER great educational theorist to develop the principles of Pestalozzi was Friedrich Froebel, the founder of the kindergarten. He and Herbart may be regarded as contemporary disciples and interpreters of the Swiss educator, who was born a generation before them, but they continued his work along rather different lines. As Herbart concerned himself with method and the work of the teacher, so Froebel laid emphasis upon the child's development and activities. The latter was perhaps a more logical successor of Pestalozzi, whose immediate pupil and colleague he had been, but he, too, worked out more broadly and explicitly the implications of the master, and attempted to interpret them after the philosophy and science of the times. Moreover, he developed his system for a period of life totally untouched by Pestalozzi, and formulated principles and methods that have come to underlie every stage of education in modern times.

Froebel's Early Life and His Experience at Jena

Froebel was permanently impressed *Friedrich Wilhelm August Froebel* (1782–1852) was born in Oberweissbach, a village in the Thüringian forest.

194

His father was a Lutheran clergyman, and the religious influence of the home made an ineradicable impression upon Froebel. The elder Froebel, however, was engrossed in the multitudinous cares of his scattered charge, and a little half-brother soon came to engage all the love and attention of the boy's stepmother. Froebel's childhood was consequently neglected, and he spent much time roving about the mysterious woods, and pondering on the birds, wild animals, plants, flowers, and the various phenomena of nature. Thus there grew within him that vein of mysticism and search for hidden unity which afterward entered so profoundly into his educational theories. This desire to find a 'connectedness' in all things was increased by the sporadic nature and the isolation from life that were only too apparent in what little formal schooling he did receive. At fifteen he was for two years apprenticed to a forester, and, although his master could not afford him proper instruction, the youth was enabled to continue his religious communion with nature. He enlarged his wood lore and practical acquaintance with plants, and gained some scientific knowledge of botany through books borrowed from a physician in the neighborhood.

At length, Froebel's hunger for a knowledge of the natural sciences impelled him to overcome parental opposition and enter the university at Jena. This institution had become the intellectual center of Germany, and the

by his religious training; and his lonely life in the forest started his mysticism and his search for 'unity' and 'connectedness.'

Going to the University of Jena, he was affected

by the ideal-
istic philos-
ophy, ro-
manticism,
and ad-
vanced atti-
tude in sci-
ence.

atmosphere was charged with the idealistic philosophy, the romantic movement, and the evolutionary attitude in science. Although Froebel was at Jena for the purpose of pursuing more practical subjects, he could not well have escaped the discussions upon Fichtian philosophy, which were current upon the street, at the table, and in every informal place of meeting, and he must have witnessed the academic growth of Fichte's pupil and colleague, Schelling. He must likewise have fallen under the spell of the Jena romanticists, — the Schlegels, Tieck, and Novalis, and possibly even of their friends and protectors, Goethe and Schiller. The advanced attitude in science at Jena must also have impressed the youth. While much of the science instruction failed to make clear that inner relation and mystic unity for which he sought, he must occasionally have caught glimpses of it in the lectures of the professors. Unhappily, after a couple of years, all this enchanted world was closed to him through financial difficulties not altogether his own fault, and he returned home in scholastic disgrace and disillusionment.

His Adoption of Teaching and Stay with Pestalozzi

Leaving the
university in
disgrace, he
groped for an
occupation,
until,
through a
Dr. Grüner,

For the next four years, Froebel was wandering and groping for a niche in life. He tried one occupation after another in keeping with his preparation — agriculture, land-surveying, clerical work in forestry, and management of country estates—but managed now and then to

absorb philosophy and romanticism and indulge his liter- *he stumbled upon his life work of teaching.*
ary impulse. Eventually, in 1805, while beginning the
study of architecture in Frankfurt, he met Dr. Anton
Grüner, head of a Pestalozzian model school, who persuaded him of his fitness for teaching and gave him a
position in the institution. Of the result Froebel declared: "From the first I found something I had always
longed for, but always missed; as if my life had at last
discovered its native element. I felt as happy as a fish
in water."

But it was soon evident to the new teacher that he *After three years of teaching in Frankfurt, he studied with Pesta- lozzi at Yverdun and learned much about physiog- raphy, music, and the play of children.*
had a sufficient knowledge of neither subject-matter nor
the laws of mental development to achieve much success
in his chosen profession. Five days after his appointment he paid a brief visit to Pestalozzi at Yverdun, and
upon his return undertook a systematic study of Pestalozzianism under the guidance of Grüner. He also began
in this period to develop his own principles and methods,
and, through the use of modeling in paper, pasteboard,
and wood with some private pupils, came to see the value
of the creative instinct as a means of education. After
three years in Frankfurt he withdrew for further study
and practice at Yverdun. The two years he spent there
proved most profitable. He gained much from the training in physiography and nature study that he gave the
pupils during long walks in the country; he found an
opportunity to study the play of children in its effect

upon intellectual as well as physical development; he first came to attach importance to that earliest training of a child by its mother; and his knowledge of music, which was to play so important a part in his methods, was greatly enlarged. Moreover, he came to feel that the lack of organization and the deficiency in unity and connection of studies that were always evident in Pestalozzi's work were an evidence of vagueness in aim and method, and he determined to eliminate these faults by making more definite the underlying principles of his master.

Crystallization of His Law of 'Unity' at Berlin

He then renewed his university studies, especially mineralogy, under Weiss at Berlin, and crystallized his mystic law of unity.

As a further result of his stay in Yverdun, Froebel began to see more than ever the need of a broader training, if he were going to unify education, and as soon as possible he gave up his work in Frankfurt, and renewed his university studies. He went first to Göttingen in 1811, but was the next year attracted to Berlin by the reputation of Professor Weiss in mineralogy. While with Weiss, he became fully "convinced of the demonstrable connection in all cosmic development," and thus crystallized that mystic law of unity with which he had long been struggling. Of this he declared : —

"What I had recognized in things great or noble, in the life of man and in the ways of God, as serving towards the development of the human race, I found I could here recognize also in the smallest of these fixed forms which Nature alone had shaped. . . . And thereafter my rocks and crystals served me as a mirror wherein I might discern mankind, and man's development and history."

For about a year the work of Froebel was interrupted by service in the army to repel the Napoleonic aggressions. Here he met his enthusiastic young friends and lifelong assistants, Heinrich Langethal and Wilhelm Middendorf, who had been students of theology at Berlin. Then, in 1814, he returned to the university, and, as an assistant to Professor Weiss, for a time became completely immersed in crystallography as a key to the organization of the universe.

His School at Keilhau and the *Education of Man*

But Froebel had never lost sight of his original purpose of educational reform. While at the university he continued his study of child nature by teaching in the Pestalozzian school of Plamann,[1] and his insight into natural science only intensified his belief in the possibility of "a more human, related, affiliated, connected treatment and consideration of the subjects of education." He declined a professorship at Stockholm, and, in 1816, against the advice of his friendly chief, he even resigned from Berlin, to take charge of the education of five young nephews and thus work out his pedagogical theories. In this venture he was soon joined by Middendorf and Langethal, and with them he founded 'The Universal German Institute of Education' at the Thürin-

In 1816, with Langethal and Middendorf, he started his 'Universal German Institute' at Keilhau.

[1] See footnote on p. 156.

Here he trained his pupils to self-expression through play, construction, nature study, and romances and ballads;

gian village of Keilhau.[1] The education here aimed to develop the pupils harmoniously in all their powers through the exercise of their own activity in subjects whose relations with one another and with life had been carefully thought out. Self-expression and free development were the watchwords of the school. Much of the training was obtained through play, and, except that the pupils were older, the germ of the kindergarten was already present. There was much practical work in the open air, in the garden about the schoolhouse, and in the building itself. The lads built dams and mills, fortresses and castles, and searched the woods for animals, birds, insects, and flowers. They learned to work out practical problems in form and number, and had the world of imagination opened to them through romances, ballads, and war songs.

and, to popularize his principles,

To popularize the Institute, Froebel published in 1826 a complete account of the theory practiced at Keilhau in his famous *Education of Man*.[2] While this work is

[1] *Die allgemeine deutsche Erziehungsanstalt.* It was first located at Griesheim, where Froebel's deceased brother, the father of three of the pupils, had been pastor, but the following year the widow bought a small property at Keilhau and the 'Institute' was moved there with her household.

[2] The title in full is: *Die Menschenerziehung, die Erziehungs-, Unterrichts-, und Lehrkunst, angestrebt der allgemeinen deutschen Erziehungsanstalt zu Keilhau, dargestellt von dem Vorsteher derselben, F. W. A. Froebel. I Band bis zum begonnenen Knabenalter.* Froebel intended to carry the 'education of man' also through youth, but he never found time to go beyond this period of early boyhood.

compressed, repetitious, and vague, and its doctrines had afterward to be corrected by experience, it contains the most systematic statement of his educational philosophy that Froebel ever made. It consists in an application to education of the idealistic philosophy and the evolutionary theory of the time. It describes Froebel's interpretation of the universe and the consequent meaning of human life, makes an exposition of his chief principles of education, and applies them to the various stages of life and to the chief school subjects.

in 1826 published his Education of Man.

But the times were not ripe for such radical positions, and the *Education of Man* influenced but few people in their estimate of the Keilhau community or the doctrines of Froebel. The Institute was even suspected of revolutionary tendencies, and the government inspector of schools was ordered to investigate. This official,[1] however, made a most favorable report, saying in part : —

"I found here a closely united family of some sixty members held together in mutual confidence and every member seeking the good of the whole. . . . That this union must have the most salutary influence on instruction and training and on the pupils themselves, is self-evident. . . . No slumbering power remains unawakened; each finds the stimulus it needs in so large a family. . . . The aim of the institution is by no means knowledge and science merely, but free self-active development of the mind from within."

[1] This discriminating inspector was a Dr. Zeh.

His Work in Switzerland

Unjust suspicions and Froebel's own failings eventually produced financial disasters, and Froebel transferred his work to Switzerland.

Nevertheless, gossip and detraction did not cease, and a disloyal assistant added fuel to the flames. Froebel, moreover, was dogmatic and irascible, and possessed little practical sense. While a financial crisis was for a time averted, the school soon found itself in serious straits. Froebel, meanwhile, strove to secure some place where he might not only rehabilitate himself, but even extend his work and give it a firmer basis.[1] Finally, a friend [2] offered his castle at Wartensee in the canton of Lucerne as the seat for the new educational institute, and in 1832 the reformer began his work in Switzerland.[3] The castle was soon found unsuitable, and Froebel accepted an invitation to locate in the neighboring town of Willisau. Here he met with bitter opposition from the conservative clergy of the vicinity, but, at a public examination held in 1833, his work was shown to be a striking success and his

---

[1] It was during this period of uncertainty that Froebel wrote the outline of what he had been attempting in his *Letter to the Duke of Meiningen* (1827) and his *Letter to Krause* (1828), the Göttingen philosopher, and from these autobiographical works most of our ideas concerning his early life have been derived. He expected at one time to be granted the estate of the duke at Helba for his enlarged school, but the offer was to a large extent withdrawn, and Froebel in anger broke off negotiations.

[2] Schnyder of Frankfurt, a pupil of Pestalozzi and a composer of music.

[3] The school at Keilhau was meanwhile left in charge of Barop, a relative of Middendorf, and under his prudent administration soon recovered all its prosperity.

reputation as an educationalist became firmly established. In 1835 the progressive government of Berne induced him to come to the castle of Burgdorf, where Pestalozzi had been, and start training courses for teachers of the canton.

The 'Kindergarten' at Blankenburg and the *Mother and Play Songs*

It was while conducting a model school at Burgdorf that it became more obvious to Froebel that "all school education was yet without a proper initial foundation, and that, until the education of the nursery was reformed, nothing solid and worthy could be attained." Through his friend, the idealistic philosopher, Krause, the *School of Infancy* of Comenius [1] had been called to his attention and "the necessity of training gifted and capable mothers" had been growing upon him. The educational importance of play now appealed to him more strongly than ever. He began to study and devise playthings, games, songs, and bodily movements that would be of value in the development of small children, although at first he did not organize his materials into a system. Two years later, however, when his wife's failing health compelled him to return to Germany, he established a regular school for children between the ages of three and

While at Burgdorf, he began to devise playthings, games, songs, and movements as a means of training; and in 1837 he started his 'Kindergarten' at Blankenburg, and six years later published his Mother and Play Songs.

[1] For Comenius and *The School of Infancy*, see pp. 33 f.

seven, which should furnish "such a course of training as would answer to the laws of development and the laws of life." The institution was located at Blankenburg, two miles from Keilhau, in one of the most romantic spots in the Thüringian Forest, and was before long appropriately christened *Kindergarten*.[1] Here he put into use the material he had invented in Switzerland, added new devices, and developed his system. The main features of this were the 'play songs' for mother and child; the series of six 'gifts,' consisting of the sphere, cube, and other geometrical forms; and the 'occupations,' which applied to different constructions the principles the child had learned through the 'gifts.' To this, during his seven years in Blankenburg, he constantly added new material, of which accounts periodically appeared in his journals.[2] By 1843 he had thus expanded his collection of songs into that attractive and popular book known as *Mother and Play Songs*.[3] This work was intended to illustrate concretely the principles and methods suggested in the *Education of Man*.

[1] That is to say, a 'garden' in which 'children' are the unfolding plants. Froebel at first called the institution by the cumbersome and uneuphonious name of *Kleinkinderbeschäftigungsanstalt* or *Anstalt für Kleinkinderpflege*, and the term *Kindergarten* came to him like an inspiration one day while walking in the forest.

[2] These articles in his *Sonntagsblatt* and *Wochenblatt* were later collected and published under the title of *Pädagogik des Kindergartens*.

[3] *Mutter- und Kose-Lieder*, which grew out of an original *Koseliedchen*.

The Closing Days of Froebel

Although the kindergarten attracted considerable attention, and many teachers came to Blankenburg to study the system, Froebel's want of practical judgment eventually involved him in a heavy debt while endeavoring to spread his gospel.[1] In consequence, the institution was obliged, in 1844, to close its doors. The next five years Froebel spent largely in traveling about Germany and lecturing upon his system, with much success, especially before groups of mothers and women teachers. But in 1849 he settled down near the famous mineral springs at Liebenstein in Saxe-Meiningen, and shortly afterward married his favorite kindergartner.[2] During this period Froebel obtained the friendship and support of the Baroness Berthe von Marenholtz-Bülow, who had come to the watering place for recuperation. This intelligent and accomplished lady became his ardent disciple. She brought a large number of people of distinction in the political and educational world to see his work in

His want of financial judgment forced him to close the school, but, after five years of lecturing, he settled again at Liebenstein.

Through Baroness von Bülow, he here made many influential friends, but in 1852 Prussia issued

---

[1] He undertook to organize a stock company, which should establish at Blankenburg a model kindergarten, a training school, a factory for kindergarten materials, and a kindergarten publishing house. The shares were to be taken by German women, who have little control of the purse strings, and the visionary scheme was doomed to failure from the start.

[2] His first wife had died in 1839. Luise Levin, his second wife, was an unlettered country girl, who, from a secret devotion to Froebel, entered menial service at Keilhau in 1845, to be near him, and although well along in her thirties, succeeded in securing a kindergarten training.

a decree
against
kinder-
gartens, and
Froebel died
under the
strain.

operation, and secured a magnificent seat for his institution upon the neighboring estate of Marienthal. She has
also given us a most interesting and accurate account of
Froebel's activities during the last thirteen years of his
life, and after his death she spread his principles throughout most of Europe. Owing to her, Froebel's closing
days bade fair to be most happy and successful, but in
1852, through a confusion of his principles with the social-
istic doctrines of his nephew, a decree was promulgated
in Prussia by the minister of education,[1] closing all
kindergartens there. While his work could still be carried
on in the other states of Germany, Froebel never recovered from this unjust humiliation. His health broke
under the strain, and he died within the year.

Development of Froebel's Principles

Froebel's
principles
grew out of
his boyhood
experiences,
and out of
the idealism,
romanticism,
and scientific
thought of
his times.

Such, in brief, is the historical development of Froebel's
theories, as they were expanded and corrected by application to practical teaching, and came to their culmination in the kindergarten. His underlying principles are
clearly the outgrowth of the religious influences of his
boyhood and his early communion with nature, combined
with the idealistic philosophy, the romantic movement,
and the scientific spirit of the day. This may be seen by
glancing at these spiritual tendencies in his times. The
chief feature of German idealism is an interpretation of

[1] Strangely enough, this bigot was the great educationalist, von Raumer.

the universe that holds to the unity of nature with the soul of man.   The 'Absolute,' or God, is regarded as the self-conscious spirit from which originated both man and nature.[1]   Hence has arisen in the universe a manifoldness within unity.   Likewise romanticism, which characterized the literature, art, and religion of the period, is mystic in expression and symbolic in thought.   It is synthetic rather than analytic in its view-point, and appeals to faith as upon a par with reason.   Finally, in the scientific thought of the times there is apparent a feeling of unity and inner relation.[2]   These influences touched the life of Froebel at every point, and made a profound impression upon one of his temperament and experience. Besides his associations at Jena, he listened to Fichte again at Berlin, and here found enthusiastic students of that philosopher in his co-workers, Langethal and Middendorf.   These friends, in turn, encouraged him to wed that brilliant idealist and romanticist,[3] who, as his wife, greatly influenced his earlier career.   Similarly, the scientific views of Jena [2] were developed in his experiences while the pupil of Weiss.   It is, therefore, but natu-

[1] See footnote on p. 208.

[2] See p. 196.   One of the science lecturers at Jena seems to have had ideas about the "interrelations of all animals" and to have foreshadowed Darwinism in his conception of man as "but a more developed type which all the lower forms are striving to realize."

[3] Henriette Wilhelmine Klepper (née Hoffmeister), the daughter of a Prussian Councilor of War.

ral that we should find Froebel adopting an organic and unitary view of life, symbolism and mysticism in expression, and the conception of ordered evolution, and that, while his writings are scientific in form, they should appear vague, emotional, and difficult to comprehend.[1]

He holds to organic 'unity' in the universe, His fundamental view of organic unity appears in his general conception of the universe, and the *Education of Man* opens with the statement: —

> "In all things there lives and reigns an eternal law. . . . This law has been and is enounced with equal clearness and distinctness in nature (the external), in the spirit (the internal), and in life, which unites the two. This all-controlling law is necessarily based on an all-pervading, energetic, living, self-conscious, and hence eternal Unity. . . . This Unity is God. All things have come from the Divine Unity, from God, and have their origin in the Divine Unity, in God alone. All things live and have their being in and through the Divine Unity, in and through God. The divine effluence that lives in each thing is the essence of each thing."

'Unity,' 'Continuity,' and 'Development' as Educational Ideals

From this Froebel derives his educational aim. Education with him "consists in a recognition of the eternal law, — its origin, essence, totality, connection, and in-

---

[1] Froebel is unconsciously following Schelling, when he talks of nature, symbolism, or æsthetics; and Fichte, when he deals with will, duty, personality, and morality. Most striking is his resemblance to Schelling, especially as he seems to have borrowed much even of his phraseology from the pupil of Schelling, his friend Krause.

tensity, and the representation and practice of it in the life of man." And in keeping with the definition, he holds in detail : —

"The purpose of education is to raise man into free, conscious obedience to the divine principle that lives in him, and to a free representation of this principle in his life. It should lead man to see that this principle also constitutes the essence of nature and is permanently manifested in nature. It should demonstrate that the same law rules both nature and man, and that man and nature proceed from God and are conditioned by him. It should lead and guide him to clearness concerning himself, to peace with nature, and to unity with God. The inner essence of things is recognized by the innermost spirit of man through outer manifestations, and all education, all instruction and training, start from the outer manifestations of man and things, and, proceeding from the outer, act upon the inner, and form its judgments concerning the inner."

which gives rise to his aim in education;

As a corollary to this principle of 'unity,' Froebel holds to 'continuity' and 'development' in all creation, and so in the human race. "God," he declares, "creates and works productively in uninterrupted *continuity*." And again, he says : "God never grafts in the world of nature, nor is the soul of man to be grafted. God *develops* the most minute and imperfect elements, through ever-rising stages, according to a law eternally founded in itself, and ever unfolding out of its own nature." This progressive development from the lower to the higher grades of being, Froebel finds equally in the advancement of the

and to 'continuity' and 'development' in all creation,

P

in the history
of the indi-
vidual, race and in the history of the individual. For this reason, while he does not formulate any set 'culture epoch' theory, like that of the Herbartians, he holds that "each successive generation and each successive human being, inasmuch as he would understand the past and present, must pass through all preceding phases of human development and culture," and he vigorously opposes "sharp limits and definite subdivisions within the continuous series of the years of development, which withdraw from attention the permanent continuity." More explicitly he maintains : —

"It is highly pernicious to consider the stages of human development — infant, child, boy or girl, man or woman — as really distinct,[1] and not, as life shows them, as continuous in themselves in unbroken transitions. . . . The child should be viewed and treated with reference to all stages of development and age, without breaks and omissions; the vigorous and complete development of each successive stage depends on the vigorous, complete, and characteristic development of each and all preceding stages of life. The boy has not become a boy, nor has the youth become a youth, by reaching a certain age, but only by having lived through childhood, and, further on, through boyhood, true to the requirements of his mind, his feelings, and his body. *The child, the boy, the man, indeed should know no other endeavor but to be at every stage of development wholly what this stage calls for.*"

Similarly, this Froebelian law of 'unity' appears in every aspect of educational theory under a variety of

[1] Contrast Rousseau's four set divisions of Emile's life. See pp. 86 ff. and 102.

guises. It is almost too comprehensive in its various applications, meanings, and implications to be fitly named by any one word or phrase. Besides elaborating the unity in the universe, nature, humanity, individual man, and age periods, Froebel insists upon a unity in the intellectual, physical, and moral life of the individual at all stages, and in the relations of his mental phases of knowing, feeling, and willing.

in intellectual, physical, and moral life, and in knowing, feeling, and willing.

'Connectedness' of All Education

He likewise holds to a unity in subject-matter and a 'connectedness' in the course of study, although he does not, with the Herbartians, crystallize any definite plan of 'correlation' or 'concentration.' For instance, he declares : —

"Human education requires the knowledge and appreciation of religion, nature, and language in their intimate living reciprocity and mutual interaction. Without the knowledge and appreciation of the intimate unity of the three, the school and we ourselves are lost in the fallacies of bottomless, self-provoking diversity."

He likewise insists upon 'connectedness' between all the subjects of the course of study, because of a feeling of dependence upon a higher being,

This integral unity should exist, Froebel holds, because of a feeling of dependence upon a higher being. Nature study gives acquaintance with the handiwork and manifestation of God, mathematics makes clear the reign of law in the universe, and language must be connected with religious instruction, in order that words may be joined with real ideas in life. So writing is but an expression of real ideas, reading should arise from a desire to recall what has been written, and art is a striving to represent the inward life. Knowledge is a tree upon which the new subjects spring as shoots from the established trunk and branches, and all compose one organic whole. And

and between
school and
home life.

there should likewise be a 'connectedness' between the school and home life, unless the former is to be regarded as a means of cramming children's minds with extraneous and external information and culture, — 'far-fetched, veneered, knowledge and skill,' instead of raising knowledge and skill, like a plant, from within. The home and the school are to work together in training the child, and the means of education should combine domestic and scholastic occupations.

'Self-activity' and 'Creativeness' as the Methods of Education

These are a few of the applications of Froebel's fundamental principle of 'unity.' Probably the most characteristic and fruitful consequence of this law was its implication as to the proper procedure in education. Froebel sums up his general method under the term 'self-

His general
method is
that of
'self-activity,'

activity,' and explains it after his usual mystic fashion. Since the divine effluence is the essence of each thing, and it is the destiny and life work of all things to reveal their essence, man, as an intelligent and rational being, should strive to become fully conscious of the divine effluence in him and reveal it with self-determination and freedom. "For the living thought," says Froebel, "the eternal divine principle as such demands and requires free *self-activity* on the part of man, the being created for freedom in the image of God." [1]   And later, in speaking of 'development,' he adds : —

"This should be brought about, not in the way of dead imitation or mere copying, but in the way of living, spontaneous *self-activity*. . . . In every human being, as a member of humanity and as a child of God, there lies and lives humanity as a whole; but in each one it is realized and expressed in a wholly particular, peculiar, personal, and unique manner, and it should be exhibited in each individual human being in this wholly peculiar, unique manner." [2]

By 'self-activity' Froebel, therefore, means more than mere activity. It is not simply activity in response to suggestion or instruction from parents or teachers that he seeks, but activity of the child in carrying out his own impulses and decisions. Individuality must be developed by this activity, and selfhood given its rightful place as the guide to the child's powers when exercised in learning. It is not sufficient that the learner shall do all for himself, but activity must enlist the entire self in all its phases of being. Development is produced through the exercise of function, which consists in the unfolding of a system of inner aims. The soul does not so much possess activity as it is itself activity, and instead

[1] *Education of Man*, § 9.   [2] *Op. cit.*, § 16.

of being influenced by, or conforming to, its environment, it tends to make its environment more and more the instrument of self-realization. Training, therefore, should begin with the internal tendencies and volitions of the pupil, but, through the activities stimulated and the interest guaranteed thereby, the instructional process should aim to direct him toward ideals and achievements of greater importance and permanence than would result from these impulses, if left to themselves. However, this increasing self-realization or individualization is also a process of socialization. It is bound up with participation in institutional life. Each one of the various human institutions in which the mentality of the race has manifested itself — the home, the school, the Church, the State, and society at large — becomes a medium for the activity of the individual, and at the same time a means of social control. Each institution has its own function, but tends to complement all the others. The individual can be educated only in the company of other human beings. Hence, Froebel held that in education 'self-activity' should be used to enable the child to enter into the life about him and to find the connection between himself and the activities of others. As far as he enters into the surrounding life, he is to receive the development needed for the present, and thereby also to be prepared for the future. Likewise, the power of execution is developed in connec-

which is both a process of self-realization and of socialization;

tion with the increasing knowledge, and there is no gap between theory and practice.

Hence with this development through 'self-activity' is connected Froebel's educational principle of 'creativeness,' by which new forms and combinations are made and expression is given to new images and ideas.   Here also he at first gives his theory a mystic garb and states it in religious language.   He declares that "since God created man in his own image, man should create and bring forth like God; this is the high meaning, the deep significance, the great purpose of work and industry, of productive and creative activity." [1]   But when he comes to deal with constructive handwork in the school, he bases his position more upon psychological grounds and says : —

and he connects with this the principle of 'creativeness.'

"Man is developed and cultured toward the fulfillment of his destiny and mission, and is to be valued, even in boyhood, not only by what he receives and absorbs from without, but much more by what he puts out and unfolds from himself. . . . Plastic material representation in life and through doing, united with thought and speech, is by far more developing and cultivating than the merely verbal representation of ideas." [2]

The 'Play Songs,' 'Gifts,' and 'Occupations,' and Other Features

Even in the *Education of Man,* Froebel declares that the systematic use of 'self-activity' and 'creativeness' has

'Self-activity' and 'creative-

[1] *Op. cit.,* § 23.   [2] *Op. cit.,* § 94.

ness' appear in the training at Keilhau, as recorded in the *Education of Man;*

been neglected in the education of the day. He here advocates development through drawing, domestic activities, gardening, building of dams, houses, and fortresses, paper cutting, pasteboard work, modeling, and other forms of creation. As we have seen,[1] while all these means of expression were utilized at Keilhau, not until his experiment at Blankenburg were they definitely organized. In the kindergarten, 'self-activity' and 'creativeness' found complete application and concrete expression, and Froebel devoted the rest of his life to developing and describing the course of this new educational institution. The training consists of three coördinate forms of expression : (1) song, (2) movement and gesture, and (3) construction; and mingled with these and growing out of each is the use of language by the child. But these means, while separate, are intended to coöperate with and interpret one another, and the process is connected as an organic whole. For example, when the story is told or read, it is expressed in song, dramatized in movement and gesture, and illustrated by a construction from blocks, paper, clay, or other material by modeling or drawing. By thus embodying the ideas in objective form, imagination and thought are to be stimulated, the eye and hand trained, the muscles coördinated, and the motives and sentiments elevated and strengthened.

but were more completely applied in the (1) song, (2) movement and gesture, and (3) construction of the kindergarten.

The best illustration of Froebel's

[1] See pp. 199 f. and 203 f.

The *Mother and Play Songs* [1] were believed by Froebel
to contain the best illustration of his system.   Of them
he says, "I have here laid down the fundamental ideas
of my educational principles."   This work consists of an
organized series of carefully selected songs, games, and
pictures, and is intended to make clear and direct the
educational instinct of the mother.   The songs should
enable her to see that the child's education begins at
birth, and should awaken her to the responsibility of
motherhood.   They should likewise exercise the infant's
senses, limbs, and muscles, and, through the loving union
between mother and child, draw both into intelligent and
agreeable relations with the common objects of life about
them.   For the culture of the maternal consciousness,
Froebel prefixed to the 'play songs' seven 'mother's
songs,' in which he depicts the mother's feelings in viewing
her new-born infant, and her hopes and fears as she wit-
nesses the unfolding physical and mental life of the child.
The fifty 'play songs' contain each three parts: (1) a
motto for the guidance of the mother; (2) a verse with
the accompanying music, to sing to the child; and (3) a
picture illustrating the verse.   Each song is also connected with some simple exercise, which answers to a
special physical, mental, or moral need of the child.
The selection and order of the songs were determined
with reference to the child's development, which ranges

[1] See p. 204.

*system is
found in the
Mother and
Play Songs.*

from the most spontaneous movements up to his ability to represent his perceptions with drawings.[1] A more complete commentary is afforded by the 'closing thoughts' and the 'explanations' furnished by Froebel at the end of the work.[2]

The most original and striking of the kindergarten materials are the so-called 'gifts' and 'occupations.'[3] The distinction between these two types of media is rather arbitrary, as they are so closely connected in use. The 'occupations' represent activities, while the 'gifts' furnish ideas for these activities. The 'gifts' combine and rearrange certain definite material, but do not change the form, while the 'occupations' reshape, modify, and transform their material. The products obtained from the one are transient, but from the other are more permanent. The emphasis in kindergarten practice has come to be transferred from the 'gifts' to the 'occupations,' which

The most original of the materials are the 'gifts' and 'occupations.'

---

[1] The 'play songs' are divided into four groups according to their content: (1) spontaneous movements and the psychology of early childhood; (2) classification of objects according to number, form, and size; (3) ideas of the heavenly bodies ('light songs'); and (4) development of the moral sense.

[2] For a description of the songs, see especially Wiggin and Smith's *Kindergarten Principles and Practice*, pp. 42–61 and 92–108; or White's *Educational Ideas of Froebel*, Chap. IX. Frances and Emily Lord have rendered the *Mutter und Kose-lieder* into English under the title *Mother's Songs, Games, and Stories*, while Susan E. Blow has translated *The Songs and Music* and *The Mottoes and Commentaries* in separate volumes.

[3] See p. 204.

have been largely increased in range and number. Froebel also strove to carry out his principle of 'development' in the order and gradation of the 'gifts.' They are so arranged as to lead from the properties or activities of one to those of the next, and, while introducing new impressions, repeat the old. Every new 'gift' is used alternately with the old, and the use of the new makes the play with the old freer and more intelligent. The first 'gift' consists of a box of six woolen balls of different colors. They are to be rolled about in play, and thus develop ideas of color, material, form, motion, direction, and muscular sensibility. A sphere, cube, and cylinder of hard wood compose the second 'gift.' Here, therefore, are found a known factor in the round sphere and an unknown one in the cube. A comparison is made of the stability of the cube with the movability of the sphere, and the two are harmonized in the cylinder, which possesses the characteristics and powers of each. The third 'gift' is a large wooden cube divided into eight equal cubes, thus teaching the relations of the parts to the whole and to one another, and making possible original constructions, such as armchairs, benches, thrones, doorways, monuments, or steps. The three following 'gifts' divide the cube in various ways so as to produce solid bodies of different types and sizes, and excite an interest in number, relation, and form. The way is thus prepared for constructive geometry, algebra, and trigonometry, and for artistic constructions. In addition to the six regular 'gifts,' additional play with 'tablets,' 'sticks,' and 'rings,' sometimes known as 'gifts' seven to nine, was also introduced by Froebel. This material introduces surfaces, lines, and points in contrast with the preceding solids, and brings out the relations of area, outline, and circumference to volume. It offers innumerable opportunities for the invention of symmetrical patterns and artistic design.[1]

The 'occupations,' which apply to practice what has been assimilated through the 'gifts,' comprise a long list of constructions with paper, sand, clay, wood, and other materials. These require greater manual dexterity and include considerable original design. They should not be undertaken until after the 'gifts,' as one must be conscious of ideas before attempting to express them. Corresponding with the 'gifts' that deal with solids may be grouped 'occupations' in clay modeling, cardboard cutting, paper folding, and wood carving; and with those of surfaces may be associated mat and paper weaving, stick shaping, sewing, bead threading, paper pricking, and drawing.[2]

---

[1] Pictures of the 'gifts' and a more complete account of their use can be found in Froebel's *Pedagogics of the Kindergarten* (translated by Jarvis), Chaps. IV–XIII; White's *Educational Ideas of Froebel*, Chap. VIII; Wiggin and Smith's *Froebel's Gifts;* and especially Kraus-Bölte's *Kindergarten Guide*, First Volume.

[2] An excellent account of the 'occupations' is given in Wiggin and Smith's *Froebel's Occupations*, and even greater details in Kraus-Bölte's *Kindergarten Guide*, Second Volume.

Nature study always formed part of Froebel's cur- riculum. His principles of unity and the symbolic rev- elation of God in nature impelled him to introduce the children early to an informal study of the natural sci- ences. Even in the school at Keilhau [1] there were con- tinual excursions for the study of nature. Likewise, the songs, games, and stories of the kindergarten are filled with references to natural surroundings, and the pupils are encouraged in their instinctive love for flowers and living creatures through gardening and the care of pet animals. These occupations satisfy their inherent crav- ings, call forth love, wonder, self-control, and self-sacri- fice, and furnish material for the development of obser- vation and intelligence. The children gain a permanent interest in natural science, become familiarized with the phenomena of nature, and come to feel a communion and living connection with God.

Since Froebel held to the method of 'self-activity' and 'creativeness' and appealed more to individual interests, his idea of discipline necessarily varied from the authori- tative one usually imposed. He held that the principle to be observed was a harmony between spontaneity and self-control. He would have evil overcome by starva- tion and atrophy and by the nurture and development of the good. He believed that the will could thus be diverted without paralyzing it, and that, if bad traits

[1] See pp. 200 and 216.

were not entirely removed, their proportion would at least be reduced. With him·punishment was not abolished, but the necessity of it practically disappeared.

The schooling beyond the kindergarten stage was never worked out by Froebel. He felt that the continuity and development in the life of the individual should be unbroken, and in the *Education of Man* he promises at some future time to consider the stages of education beyond boyhood, with which he closes there. But after the kindergarten was once formulated, he became completely absorbed in the development of early childhood, and could not be induced for any length of time to take an interest in the later stages of education and the ordinary school problems. In consequence, except for a small effort of Froebel toward the close of his life to map out a course for 'transition classes,' no one has ever seriously undertaken to bridge the gap between the kindergarten activities, connected with physical development and sense impressions, and the elementary school, which concerns itself more with judgment, reasoning, and abstractions.

Froebel's Crudities, Mysticism, and Symbolism

For one pursuing destructive criticism only, it would not be difficult to find flaws in both the theory and practice of Froebel. In fact, the defects in both his typical works, *Education of Man* and *Mother and Play Songs*, are

singularly obtrusive, if they be regarded only superficially. *Play Songs are crude;*
In the latter the pictures are rough and poorly drawn,
the music is crude,[1] the verses are difficult to memorize,
and the arrangement and sequence seem at times to lack
consistency.   But the illustrations and songs served
well the interests and needs of those for whom they were
produced, and Froebel himself was not insistent that
they should be used after more satisfactory compositions
were found.[2]   He wished only to afford examples of how
the mother might aid in the development of her child,
and no other collection of children's songs has ever
been devised to compare with his in educational value.
Similarly, the mysticism, artificiality, and even triviality *and his mysticism, symbolism,*
that appear in various forms throughout the *Education*
of Man bear no essential relation to his basal principles *and artificiality*
or his argument.   In undertaking to make apparent *are fantastic, vague, and*
and efficient at every point the fundamental law of life *confusing;*
and development, Froebel often strains his principle of
'unity,' and becomes most vague and fanciful.   Such,
for example, would seem to be his constant attempts to
reveal the relationship underlying apparent conflict in
his 'harmonization of opposites' and his 'connection by

[1] It was composed for most of the songs by his disciple, Robert Kohl.

[2] However, despite the different interests and occupations of American
life and the advance in knowledge and music, there is a group of Froebe-
lians in this country that adheres to the letter rather than the spirit
of the master.

contrasts.' [1] So symbolism is overemphasized by him, and is often fantastic and confusing, especially when the basal philosophy is not understood. Since all things live and have their being in and through God and the divine principle in each is the essence of its life, everything is liable to be considered by Froebel as symbolic in its very nature and as made by God to reveal and express himself. Thus with him the sphere becomes the symbol of diversity in unity,[2] the faces and edges of crystals all have mystic meanings,[3] and the numbers three and five reveal an inner significance.[4] At times this symbolism descends into a literal and verbal pun, where it seems as if Froebel can hardly be serious or is struggling for a suggestive system of mnemonics. Such is his explanation of the 'ball' as the symbol of unity, the 'nursling' as a great appropriating 'eye,' and the 'boy' as one who strives to 'announce' himself.[5] At times, too, Froebel's mystic views and attitude on divine revelation make a curious and incongruous combination with his

[1] See, for example, 'rest' and 'motion' in *Education of Man*, § 25.

[2] *Op. cit.*, § 69. [3] *Op. cit.*, §§ 70-72.

[4] This is seen in his description of plants and flowers, while in his treatment of the family he especially vents an eccentric disquisition on the number five.

[5] *Ball* is interpreted as *B*(ild des)*all*, *Säugling* as one who (S)*augt*, and *Kind* as the stage where he (ver)*kündigt*. See *Pedagogics of the Kindergarten*, p. 32, and *Education of Man*, §§ 20 and 28. Similarly, *op. cit.*, § 25, the 'senses' (*S-inn*) are regarded as the means of 'self-active internalization' (*Selbsthätige Inner*lichmachung).

evolutionary doctrines, and his most profound philosophy
is interspersed with marked religiosity.[1] But, after all, but these features are
these faults, striking as they are, are incidental, and incidental, and should
while they have been magnified and expanded into im- not be mag-
portant features by many of Froebel's literal disciples,[2] nified.
they should not be divorced from the real psychological
principles, upon which they are mere excrescences.
Likewise, Froebel's practical work, while at times mechanical, over-schematized, and bolstered by esoteric
speculations, is most ingenious, and has enabled society
to provide for a neglected and most important stage in
education.

The Value of His Principles

It is, at any rate, a most lamentable interpretation And, on the other hand,
that takes account only of the shortcomings of Froebel. he made Pestalozzi's
He was the truest successor of Pestalozzi. Like the 'natural develop-
Swiss reformer, he desired a natural development of man, ment' more
but he had a clearer and more definite comprehension definite, and applied ad-
of what this consisted in, and he greatly enlarged the vanced
means of accomplishing a training in keeping with it. philosophy and scien-tific ideas to
Pestalozzi, through his sympathy for humanity and the education.
inspiration of the moment, was interested primarily
in the practical aspect of educational reform, and developed his theories afterward.   Froebel, on the other hand,
sought to formulate general principles from his observa-

---

[1] See, for example, *op. cit.*, § 23.   [2] Cf. footnote on p. 223.

tion, make his educational method grow out of their application, and constantly test his generalizations by practical experience. While the one would teach the pupil to secure accurate knowledge through observation and to imitate, the other would enable him to train his senses and emotions to proper activity as a preparation for later knowledge and activity of a more original sort.

Froebel has thus not only supplemented Pestalozzi, but is recognized as one of the first reformers to apply the advanced philosophy and scientific ideas of the nineteenth century to education. While Froebel never developed his system much beyond the earliest period of life, his principles are suggestive of the most important tendencies in all stages of education to-day. Through his ideas of 'continuity' and 'development' one may more thoroughly understand the nature of the child and realize the central feature in all life relations. From these principles may be derived the real purpose of education and the means and method for accomplishing it. Thus may be secured a training adapted to every period of life and stage of development, furnishing the highest philosophy and the most ennobling ethical thought. Now that the meaning of his 'self-activity' and 'creativeness' is coming to be comprehended, they are recognized as most essential laws in the educational process, and are to be valued as the universal criterion of effective teaching. In harmony with Froebel, the

Thus he formulated principles and a training that may be adapted to any period of life.

school is coming to be conceived as an institution in which to discover and work out individuality by means of initiative and execution; and spontaneous activities, like play, constructive work, and nature study, have more and more become the means to this end. The importance of having all instruction lead to activity as directly as possible is now appreciated, and education has been given a social, moral, and practical meaning throughout the learning process. Thus the implications of Froebel's system are apparent in all modern educational theory and practice.

The Spread of Froebelianism through Europe

Froebelianism and the kindergarten, then, contained principles that were destined to spread by virtue of their educational value. But their dissemination was greatly facilitated after the death of Froebel by the reformer's devoted followers. Froebel's widow, Middendorf, and the Baroness von Bülow especially became the heirs of his spiritual possessions, and proceeded at once to make the heritage productive. Middendorf did not long survive the master, and Frau Froebel's part in the wide evangelization was somewhat limited by her education. It remained for the intellectual and cultured noblewoman, by means of her social position and knowledge of modern languages, to become the great apostle of Froebel throughout Europe. Shortly after his death,

Froebel's principles were spread by the Baroness von Bülow throughout Europe,—

having failed to obtain a revocation of the edict in Prussia from either the ministry or the king, the baroness turned to foreign lands. She visited France, Belgium, Holland, England, Italy, Russia, and nearly every other section of Europe, and the propaganda was everywhere eagerly *France,* embraced. In Paris she took rooms at the Louvre, and gave parlor lectures to audiences including the most distinguished men of all religions and philosophies, who accepted the Froebelian principles and system with remarkable unanimity. The minister of education in *Belgium,* Belgium invited the baroness to Brussels, where she addressed numerous circles of prominent women, school officers, and teachers, and by means of great personal efforts succeeded in establishing model kindergartens *Holland,* and a journal devoted to the movement. In Holland she founded kindergartens at Amsterdam, the Hague, Rotterdam, and Gueldern, and interested the minister of education, many school inspectors, and directors of schools in the maintenance of such institutions. She *England,* carried on a similar work in England, and popularized the idea throughout the British Isles; and kindergartens, endorsed by numerous men of repute, sprang up on all *and Italy;* sides. Through her lectures in Italy a system of kindergartens was started at Naples and elsewhere, and great promises of support were exacted. A most noteworthy recognition was shown the principles she represented by the invitation given her to speak before the 'Congress

of Philosophers' at Frankfurt in 1867. This distin- and laid be-
fore the
guished gathering had been called to inquire into con- 'Congress of
Philosophers'
temporary educational movements. As a result of the at Frank-
furt.
elucidation of Froebelianism by the baroness during four
afternoons of the sessions, a committee of the society,
known as the 'Froebel Union,' was formed to continue
a study of the system. Among the achievements of this
organization was the foundation five years later of an
institution for training kindergartners at Dresden.

Thus, while the kindergarten was not generally adopted Thus the
kindergarten
by the governments, it was widely established by volun- principles
have been
tary means throughout civilized Europe, and in all coun- greatly ex-
tries the work has grown to mammoth proportions. In- tended in
Europe, ex-
struction in Froebelian principles is now generally re- cept in
Germany.
quired in most normal and teacher training institutions of
Europe. Sometimes, as in France and England, it has
been combined with the infant school movement,[1] and
has lost some of its original characteristics, but even
in these cases the cross-fertilization has afforded abun-
dant educational fruitage. Only in Germany, the native

---

[1] While the infant schools originally began in France in 1769, and were
the prototypes of the *écoles maternelles*, the movement also started in
England independently a generation later through Robert Owen. This
philanthropist hoped thereby to mitigate the illiteracy of the factory
population, which was largely recruited by children from five to seven,
who were bound out for nine years before receiving any education. The
schools were especially popularized through the writings of Samuel
Wilderspin and through 'The Home and Colonial Society.'

land of the kindergarten, has serious hostility to the idea remained. The deadening effects of the ministerial decree, despite the efforts of the heroic baroness in establishing and encouraging kindergarten associations, hung over the German states for a decade; and even since the removal of the ban, kindergartens have, with few exceptions, never been recognized as real schools or part of the regular state system. The kindergartners are not subject to the requirements demanded of all other elementary teachers, and are forbidden to touch on the formal school subjects or work of any sort that would seem to duplicate the primary curriculum. Even to-day the German kindergarten is regarded as little more than a day nursery or convenient place to deposit small children, and have them amused. The educational principles for which Froebel contended are not generally conceded in Germany.[1]

The Kindergarten in the United States

The kinder-
garten has
had the wid-
est influence

The influence of the kindergarten has been more marked in the United States than in any other country. In the early sixties Elizabeth P. Peabody and others

[1] When Professor Payne of the London College of Preceptors visited the kindergartens in six German cities in 1874, he found that, while the theory was just, natural, and all-sided, the teachers were inefficient, and the rooms were often small, unsanitary, and ill-lighted. (See Payne, *Lectures on the History of Education*, pp. 203-271.) More than a generation later the same general conditions seem to obtain.

became interested in accounts of Froebel's system, and, in the United States. without a proper knowledge of the details, undertook to open kindergartens in Boston. Notwithstanding the immediate success of these institutions and the evident enjoyment of the children, Miss Peabody felt that It was introduced in she had not succeeded in getting the real principles and Boston by Elizabeth P. spirit of Froebel, and in 1867 she went to study with Peabody, in New York by his widow, who had been settled in Hamburg for several Maria years. Upon her return the following year Miss Pea- Bölte, and in St. Louis body corrected the errors in her work and established a by Susan E. Blow; and periodical to explain and spread Froebelianism. The support was given remainder of her life was spent in interesting parents, the work by S. H. Hill, philanthropists, and school boards in the movement, Mrs. Quincy and a service was done for the kindergarten in America A. Shaw, and others. almost equal to that of Baroness von Bülow in Europe. In 1872 Maria Bölte, afterwards the wife of Professor John Kraus,[1] who had studied with Frau Froebel, was induced to settle in New York, and, through her pupils and those of other German kindergartners, the cause was rapidly promoted. The same year saw the beginning of Susan E. Blow's great work in St. Louis, where her free training school for kindergartners was opened. Two years later S. H. Hill of Florence, Massachusetts, started a munificent provision for free kindergartens in his vicinity, and four years after that Mrs. Quincy A. Shaw

[1] She has since been widely known as Mrs. Maria Kraus-Bölte, and is still (1911) living in New York City.

began establishing them at various locations in the neighborhood of Boston, until she was supporting at least thirty such institutions. Many other philanthropic persons became much interested, and over one hundred voluntary associations were soon organized to found and maintain kindergartens. Through the work of Emma Marwedel, who was invited to California in 1876 by the 'Froebel Union,' successful training classes were established at Los Angeles, Oakland, and Berkeley. Voluntary kindergartens were also rapidly opened, and there was soon organized the 'Golden Gate Association' at San Francisco, which at its height supported forty-one free institutions and an excellent training school. In Philadelphia, Chicago, Milwaukee, Detroit, Pittsburg, Cincinnati, Cleveland, Washington, Baltimore, Louisville, and other centers, subscriptions were before long raised by the churches and other philanthropic agencies, and the work everywhere grew apace.

It soon became part of the public school system in St. Louis, San Francisco, Boston, and other cities. But philanthropy and private foundations, after all, are restrictive, and it was not until the kindergartens began to be adopted by the school systems that the movement became truly national in the United States. Boston early added kindergartens to her public schools, but after several years of trial gave them up on account of the expense. The first permanent establishment under a city board was made in 1873 at St. Louis through the efforts of Miss Blow and Dr. William T. Harris, then city superintendent of schools. Twelve kindergartens were organized at first, but others were opened as rapidly as competent directors could be prepared at Miss Blow's training school. Within a decade there were more than fifty public kindergartens and nearly eight thousand pupils in St. Louis. San Francisco authorized the incorporation of kindergartens in the public schools in 1880; and New York, Boston, Philadelphia, Buffalo, Pittsburg, Rochester, Providence, Milwaukee, Minneapolis, and most other progressive cities and even many smaller municipalities have gradually made the work an integral part of their system. At present there must be nearly two hundred cities that include this stage of education in their schools. That means a total of some fifteen hundred public kindergartens [1] with nearly twice as many teachers and fully one hundred thousand pupils. About twenty of the cities employ a special supervisor to inspect the work. Excellent training schools for kindergartners are also maintained by half a hundred public and quasi-public normal institutions. A large number of extensive treatises, manuals, and periodicals devoted to the subject of kindergarten work are published, and have a wide circulation in every state of the Union.[2]

[1] The number would be nearly quadrupled by the addition of the private kindergartens.

[2] A most complete, though succinct, account of the history of the kindergarten in the United States is given in Susan E. Blow's *Kindergarten Education*, pp. 1–10, under the head of 'four sharply defined movements.'

SUPPLEMENTARY READING [1]

I. Sources

*FROEBEL, F. W. A., *Autobiography* (translated by Michaelis and Moore); *Education by Development* (translated by Jarvis); *Education of Man* (translated by Hailmann); *Letters* (edited by Heinemann); *Letters on the Kindergarten* (translated by Poesche, and edited by Michaelis and Moore); *Mother Songs, Games, and Stories* (translated by F. and E. Lord); *Mottoes and Commentaries of Mother Play* (translated by Eliot and Blow); *Pedagogics of the Kindergarten* (translated by Jarvis); *Songs and Music of Mother Play* (translated by Blow).

LANGE, W. *Froebel's Gesammelte Pädagogische Schriften* (three volumes) and *Reminiscences of Froebel* (*American Journal of Education*, Vol. XXX, pp. 833–845).

*MARENHOLTZ–BÜLOW, BERTHE M. von. *Reminiscences of Friedrich Froebel*.

SEIDEL, F. *Froebel's Mutter- und Kose-Lieder*.

II. Authorities

*BARNARD, H. (Editor). *Kindergarten and Child Culture*.

*BLOW, SUSAN E. *Educational Issues in the Kindergarten, Kindergarten Education* (*Monographs on Education in the United States*, edited by N. M. Butler, No. I), *Letters to a Mother*, and *Symbolic Education*.

BOARDMAN, J. H. *Educational Ideas of Froebel and Pestalozzi*.

*BOWEN, H. C. *Froebel and Education by Self-activity*.

---

[1] For further references to the Froebelian literature, consult Bowen, *Froebel*, pp. 197–204; Cubberley, *Syllabus in the History of Education*, pp. 273 f. ; and Monroe, *Syllabus in the History and Principles of Education* (edition of 1911), pp. 66 ff.

BUCHNER, E. F.   *Froebel from a Psychological Standpoint* (*Education*, Vol. XV, pp. 105–113 and 169–173).

BUTLER, N. M.   *Some Criticisms of the Kindergarten* (*Educational Review*, Vol. XVIII, pp. 285–291).

COLE, P. R.   *Herbart and Froebel: an Attempt at Synthesis.*

*COMPAYRÉ, G.   *History of Pedagogy.*   (Translated by Payne.) Pp. 446–465.

EUCKEN, R.   *The Philosophy of Froebel* (*The Forum*, Vol. XXX, pp. 172 ff.).

GOLDAMMER, H.   *The Kindergarten.*   (Translated by Wright.)

*HAILMANN, W. N.   *Kindergarten Culture.*

HANSCHMANN, A. B.   *The Kindergarten System.*

HARRISON, ELIZABETH A.   *A Study of Child Nature.*

HERFORD, W. H.   *The Student's Froebel.*

HOPKINS, LOUISA P.   *The Spirit of the New Education.*

*HUGHES, J. L.   *Froebel's Educational Laws.*

*KRAUS–BÖLTE, MARIA, and KRAUS, J.   *The Kindergarten Guide.*   Two volumes.

MACVANNEL, J. A.   *Educational Theories of Herbart and Froebel* and *The Philosophy of Froebel* (*Teachers College Record*, Vol. IV, pp. 335–377).

MARENHOLTZ–BÜLOW, BERTHE M. VON.   *The Child and Child Nature.*

MEIKLEJOHN, J. M. D.   *The New Education.*

MUNROE, J. P.   *The Educational Ideal.*   Chap. VIII.

*PAYNE, J.   *Froebel and the Kindergarten.*

*PEABODY, ELIZABETH P.   *Education in the Home, the Kindergarten, and the Primary School* and *Lectures in the Training Schools for Kindergartners.*

POLLOCK, LOUISE.   *National Kindergarten Manual.*

POULSSON, EMILIE.   *Love and Law in Child Training.*

PROUDFOOT, ANDREA H.   *A Mother's Ideals.*

*QUICK, R. H.   *Educational Reformers.*   Chap. XVII.

SCHAEFFER, MARY F.   *A Cycle of Work in the Kindergarten.*

SHIRREFF, EMILY.   *A Short Sketch of the Life of Friedrich Froebel* and *The Kindergarten System.*

SNIDER, D. J.   *Froebel's Mother Play Songs, The Life of Froebel,* and *The Psychology of Froebel's Play Gifts.*

THORNDIKE, E. L.   *The Psychology of the Kindergarten* (*Teachers College Record,* pp. 377–408).

WEAVER, EMILY A.   *Paper and Scissors in the Schoolroom.*

WELTON, J.   *A Synthesis of Herbart and Froebel.*

*WHITE, JESSIE.   *The Educational Ideas of Froebel.*

WIGGIN, KATE D.   *Children's Rights.*

WIGGIN, KATE D. (Editor).   *The Kindergarten.*

WIGGIN, KATE D., and SMITH, NORA A.   *Froebel's Gifts, Froebel's Occupations, Kindergarten Principles and Practice,* and *The Republic of Childhood.*

CHAPTER XII

LANCASTER AND BELL, AND THE MONITORIAL SYSTEM

IN 1798, an English Quaker, but twenty years of age, opened a novel type of school for the children of the poor in Southwark, London. The youthful teacher, whose name was *Joseph Lancaster* (1778–1838), had come to feel that "the want of system and order is almost uniform in every class of schools within the reach of the poor." He declared, " there is little encouragement for masters, parents, and scholars; and while this is the case, it is no wonder that ignorance prevails among the poor." That this illiteracy and lack of organization might be overcome, he began himself to educate as many of the barefoot and unkempt children of the district as he could. His schoolroom was soon crowded with a hundred or more pupils, and, in order to teach them all, he used the older scholars as assistants. He taught the lesson first to these 'monitors,' and they in turn imparted it to the others, who were divided into equal groups. Each monitor cared for a single group.

To educate the poor in Southwark, Lancaster started a 'monitorial' school.

Success of Monitorialism, and the Formation of the 'British and Foreign' and the 'National' Societies

His success, chronicled in his *Improvements in Education,* caused the system to be spread throughout England.

The work was very successful from the first, and Lancaster called further attention to it in 1803 by an account he published under the title of *Improvements in Education as it respects the Industrious Classes of the Community.* The school was twice enlarged by persons of wealth; many of the nobility and aristocracy came to visit the institution; and the king summoned Lancaster for an interview, and made a generous contribution for his work. A training school was soon opened to spread this system among other teachers, and Lancaster began to lecture on his methods throughout England and to establish 'monitorial' schools everywhere. It was generally believed that the problem of national education had at length been solved, and that an effective means had been found for educating everyone with little cost. Lancaster, however, proved most reckless, and his venture had by 1808 plunged him into debt to the extent of six thousand pounds. Having rescued him from the debtors' prison, certain philanthropic men of means in that year founded 'The Royal Lancasterian Institution,' to continue the work on a practical basis. But within half a dozen years, Lancaster, who seems never to have been able to get along with people, withdrew from the association and started a school of his own. A few years later he left England

'The Royal Lancasterian Institution' was founded to continue his work; but Lancaster soon left England, and the association became known as 'The British and Foreign Society.'

for foreign lands, where he again met with failure and poverty, and eventually died in the city of New York, a disappointed man.

Yet the organization for perpetuating his work, which after the withdrawal of Lancaster became known as 'The British and Foreign Society,' continued to flourish and perform a splendid service for education. So successful was it that the Church of England began to fear its liberalistic influence upon education. Following the nonconformist attitude of its Quaker founder, the education of the society included religion and reading the Bible, but permitted no catechism or denominational instruction of any sort. To most Anglican churchmen such religious teaching seemed loose and colorless, and in 1811 'The National Society for Promoting the Education of the Poor in the Principles of the Established Church' was founded by them. This long-named association was to use the 'monitorial' system, and to have a Reverend Doctor Bell as its manager. *Andrew Bell* (1753–1832) had been an army chaplain and the superintendent of an orphanage in India, and had the idea of monitorial instruction suggested to him by the Hindu education. A year before Lancaster opened his school, Dr. Bell had published his treatise known as *An Experiment in Education Made at the Male Asylum of Madras;* and while the Quaker philanthropist began his system independently, it is not unlikely that he re-

To compete with this non-sectarian association, the Church of England founded 'The National Society' with Dr. Bell in charge, who had published an account of his *Experiment in Education*, on the 'monitorial' basis.

ceived help later from Bell. Although they formed no part of Bell's original methods in Madras, the catechism and the prayer book were now taught dogmatically in the schools founded by the 'National Society,' and as Dr. Bell proved an admirable director, the affairs of the organization prospered marvelously. In consequence, a healthy rivalry with the older association of the Lancasterians rapidly grew up.

Differences between the Systems of Lancaster and Bell

'Monitorial' or 'mutual' instruction, however, was not original with either Lancaster or Bell. Besides being used by the Hindus,[1] it has formed part of the Jesuit system of education,[2] and was confidently recommended by Comenius in his *Didactica Magna*.[3] Nevertheless, it was the work of Lancaster and Bell that greatly developed the method and brought it into prominence. The plans of the two men, while analogous, differed somewhat in spirit and details. Without considering the methods of religious instruction, the system of Lancaster was generally animated by broader motives. While he failed to teach certain subjects, it was simply because his resources were limited; but the National

The system of Lancaster was broader than that of the National Society, and was more elaborate.

[1] See Graves, *History of Education before the Middle Ages*, pp. 87 f.
[2] See Graves, *History of Education during the Transition*, p. 218.
[3] See pp. 32 f.

Society purposely curtailed the range of its instruction on the ground that "there is a risk of elevating those who are doomed to the drudgery of daily labour above their station, and rendering them unhappy and discontented with their lot." In the matter of details, both men worked out systematically the idea of instructing through monitors, and both used a desk covered with sand[1] as a means of teaching writing; but in other respects Lancaster elaborated the method more than Bell. By having the speller or other text printed in large type and suspending it from the wall, he made one book serve for a whole class, or even for the entire school. Through the use of slates and dictation he had five hundred boys spell and write the same word at the same time. He arranged a new method in arithmetic whereby any child who could read might teach the subject with accuracy. Moreover, although a member of the Society of Friends, Lancaster introduced more military discipline into his system than did his rival. He believed in company organization, drill, regimental control, precision, and a prompt observance of the word of command. He also developed a system of badges, tickets, offices, and other rewards, and, in order to avoid flogging, a set of punishments by which the offender was made an object of ridicule rather than physical pain. There were also a number of unessential differences between the two

[1] See footnote 1 on p. 240.

R

systems in the manner of arranging their classes.[1] They likewise differed in their method of training teachers. In order to acquire the Lancasterian system, a teacher was required to spend a week or more as a monitor in each of the classes from the lowest to the highest, while with the Bell organization he had to become an actual pupil in each of the grades.

Value of the Monitorial System in England

The monitorial system, while it accomplished much when little attention was given to education, was formal and mechanical.

Neither Bell nor Lancaster deserves much praise as an educational reformer. Each was vain and pedagogically ignorant, and saw but one side of education. While both societies accomplished much good at a time when little attention was given to instruction and less to the problems of education, the monitorial systems overemphasized repetition in the teaching process and treated education purely from the standpoint of routine. The monitorial method was not real instruction, but a formal drill. It had no principles and little of the elasticity that was apparent in the more psychological methods of the reformers on the Continent. The mechanical basis of such a system is exposed by the arith-

[1] For example, Lancaster had his pupils located in a mass at the center of the room, while Bell arranged their desks around the walls. The classes when reciting under Lancaster's monitors consisted of ten or twelve standing in semicircles; Bell placed a larger number in each group and seated them on benches in three sides of a square.

metical boast of Lancaster. He calculated: "Each boy can spell one hundred words in a morning. If one hundred scholars can do that two hundred mornings yearly, the following will be the total of their efforts at improvement." He then shows that there will be an annual achievement of two million words spelt. Similarly, in arithmetic he seems to hold that it is simply a question of the number of sums done in a given time, and not at all a matter of principles.

Yet the Lancaster-Bell schools did awaken the conscience of the English nation to the need of general education for the poor, and the system emphasized the school as an organized community for mutual aid. The societies afforded a substitute, though a poor one, for national education in the days before the government was willing to pay for general education or the denominations were able to furnish it, and they became the avenues through which such appropriations as the government did make were distributed.

But it afforded a national education in England before it could be otherwise obtained.

Results of Lancasterianism in the United States

In the United States, where complete freedom in religion obtained, the system of Dr. Bell and the National Society found little footing. The monitorial system in its Lancasterian form, however, was introduced into New York City in 1806. The 'Society for the Establishment of a Free School,' after investigating

The Lancasterian system was introduced into many American cities,

the best methods in other cities and countries, decided
to try the system of Lancaster. It spread rapidly
through New York, Pennsylvania, Massachusetts, Connecticut, and other states, and before long had influenced nearly all cities of any size as far south as
Charleston, and west as far as Cincinnati. In 1818
Lancaster himself was invited to America, and assisted
in the monitorial schools of New York, Brooklyn, and
Philadelphia. A dozen years later the system began to
be introduced into the high schools and academies, and
for two decades it was the prevailing method in secondary education. Training schools for teachers on the
Lancasterian basis became common.

and did a
great service
where free
schools had
been few

In fact, the monitorial system was destined to perform
a great service for American education. At the time of
its introduction, public and free schools were generally
lacking, outside of New England. Even in that section
the early Puritan provision for schools had largely become a dead letter, and the facilities that existed were
meager, and available during but a small portion of the
year. In all parts of the country illiteracy was almost
universal among children of the poor. This want of
school opportunities was rendered more serious by the
rapid growth of American cities, which was evident even
in the earliest part of the century, and by the consequent
increase and concentration of ignorance, poverty, and
crime. Societies like that in New York City, formed to

study and relieve the situation, were driven to the conclusion that free schools must be instituted, if the poorer classes were to be trained to habits of thrift and virtue. Because of its comparative inexpensiveness, these philanthropic associations came to regard the system of Lancaster as a very godsend for their purpose. And when, before long, the people awoke to the crying need of public education, the legislators found the monitorial schools the cheapest way out of the difficulty, and the provision they made for these schools gradually prepared the way for the ever increasing expenditures and taxation that had to be made before satisfactory schools could be established. Hence the introduction of Lancasterianism may well be considered to have provided a basis for the substantial public support of education now universal in the United States.

Moreover, the Lancasterian schools were not only economical, but most effective when the educational conditions of the times are taken into consideration. Even in the cities, the one-room and one-teacher school, which had been perpetuated from the district system, was the prevailing type, and grading was practically unknown. The whole organization and administration was shiftless and uneconomical, and a great improvement was brought about by the carefully planned and detailed methods of Lancaster. The schools were made over through his definite mechanics of instruction,

and the work ineffective,

centralized management, well-trained teachers, improved apparatus, discipline, hygiene, and other features. We can, then, well understand the enthusiasm for these new schools that is apparent in the utterances and writings of statesmen, educators, and other persons of the times that felt responsible for the training of the people. One of the earliest and best known estimates is that of the governor of New York, De Witt Clinton, who in 1809 declared in his address at the dedication of the new building of the Free School Society : —

"When I perceive that many boys in our school have been taught to read and write in two months, who did not before know the alphabet, and that even one has accomplished it in three weeks — when I view all the bearings and tendencies of this system — when I contemplate the habits of order which it forms, the spirit of emulation which it excites, the rapid improvement which it produces, the purity of morals which it inculcates — when I behold the extraordinary union of celerity in instruction and economy of expense — and when I perceive one great assembly of a thousand children, under the eye of a single teacher, marching with unexampled rapidity and with perfect discipline to the goal of knowledge, I confess that I recognize in Lancaster the benefactor of the human race. I consider his system as creating a new era in education, as a blessing sent down from heaven to redeem the poor and distressed of this world from the power and dominion of ignorance." [1]

[1] For Clinton's complete eulogy of the system adopted by the Free School Society, of which he was president, see Bourne, *History of the Public School Society of the City of New York*, pp. 18–20.

But while the monitorial methods met a great educational emergency in the United States, they were clearly mechanical, inelastic, and without psychological foundation. Naturally their sway could not last long, and as public sentiment for education increased, and enlarged material resources enabled the people to make greater appropriations for education, the obvious defects of the monitorial system became more fully appreciated and brought about its abandonment. It gave way to the more psychological conceptions of Pestalozzi and to those afterward formulated by Froebel and Herbart.

but disappeared when educational sentiment improved.

SUPPLEMENTARY READING

I. SOURCES

*BELL, A. *An Experiment in Education.*
*LANCASTER, J. *British System of Education* and *Improvements in Education.*

II. AUTHORITIES

*ADAMS, F. *History of the Elementary School Contest in England.* Pp. 44–64.
*BARNARD, H. *American Journal of Education.* Vol. X, pp. 323–531.
BARTLEY, G. C. T. *The Schools for the People; History, Development, and Present Condition.* Pp. 50–51 and 60–61.
BOURNE, W. O. *History of the Public School Society of the City of New York.* Pp. 9–20, 32, 172–173, and 687–698.
FITCH, J. G. *Educational Aims and Methods.* Lect. XI.
*GILL, J. *Systems of Education.* Pp. 162–202.

GREGORY, R. *Elementary Education.*

HOLMAN, H. *English National Education.* Chap. II.

LEITCH, J. *Practical Educationalists and their Systems.* Pp. 121–165.

*MEIKLEJOHN, J. M. D. *An Old Educational Reformer, Dr. Andrew Bell.*

OLIVER, H. K. *Advantages and Defects of the Monitorial System of Instruction.*

RANDALL, S. S. *History of the Common School System of the State of New York.* Pp. 28–32.

ROSS, G. W. *The Schools of England and Germany.* Chap. II.

*SADLER, M. E., and EDWARDS, J. W. *Summary of Statistics, Regulations, etc., of Elementary Education, England and Wales (English Education Department, Special Reports, Vol. II, pp. 436–544).*

*SALMON, D. *Joseph Lancaster.*

*SHARPLESS, I. *English Education.* Pp. 1–8.

SOUTHEY, R. and C. C. *The Life of the Rev. Andrew Bell.*

SPALDING, T. A. *The Work of the London School Board.* Pp. 13–14.

STEINER, B. C. *History of Education in Maryland.* Pp. 57–62.

STOCKWALL, T. B. *History of Public Education in Rhode Island.* Pp. 254–294.

WICKERSHAM, J. P. *History of Education in Pennsylvania.* Pp. 254–285.

WIGHTMAN, J. M. *Annals of the Boston Primary School Committee.* Pp. 35–116.

CHAPTER XIII

HORACE MANN AND THE AMERICAN EDUCATIONAL REVIVAL

THE close of the first half of the nineteenth century was distinguished by a remarkable revival in education throughout the United States. This awakening began and centered in Massachusetts, and was greatly strengthened by the leadership and efforts of Horace Mann. To appreciate the underlying causes, one must, therefore, learn something of the life and purposes of this great American educator.

The Early Career of Horace Mann

Horace Mann (1796–1859) was born on a small farm in Franklin, Massachusetts. His parents were plain people, but of superior mental capacity and considerable strength of character, and the little town in which he grew up also furnished an environment of unusually high ideals in intelligence and morals. The hard conditions of New England farm life and the early loss of his father fixed in him lifelong habits of industry, initiative, and responsibility. While the school training of the day was meager and circumscribed, he learned in his boyhood to love nature and her handiwork, and ac-

The parentage and training of Horace Mann tended to cultivate in him industry, initiative, and a reverence for knowledge.

quired a reverence for knowledge and books. He also
secured much instruction and intellectual enrichment
from the small library of his native town.[1] While he
reacted most strongly from the stern, uncompromising
Calvinism of the religious life of the times, it inculcated
in him a faith in God and a subordination of his moral
nature to the higher law, and he obtained through its

After gradua·
tion from
college,
and two
years as a
tutor,
Mann stud-
ied law, and
soon became
a legislator.

system a remarkable drill in logic. At the age of twenty,
young Mann happened upon a brilliant preparatory
teacher, and was speedily fitted to enter the sophomore
class of Brown University in the fall of the same year.
He was graduated in 1819 at the head of his class, and
was shortly afterward engaged for two years as a tutor
in Latin and Greek at his *alma mater*. After demonstrating extraordinary ability as a classical scholar and
teacher, and concluding, far in advance of his times,
that the natural sciences were much superior in content
and discipline to the classics, he turned his attention to
the study of law [2] as a profession and of metaphysics

---

[1] This library was presented to the town by Benjamin Franklin, for
whom the place was named. He requested his friend, Dr. Richard Price
of London, to purchase to the amount of twenty-five pounds such books
as would foster sound religion and government.

[2] Mann studied at the famous law school of Judge Gould in Litchfield,
Connecticut, which, during its existence of less than half a century, graduated sixteen United States senators, fifty members of Congress, five
cabinet officers, several foreign ministers, and innumerable justices of the
federal and higher state courts.

as an avocation. As a practitioner he impressed every one with his conscientiousness [1] as much as with his knowledge of the law and his logic and eloquence. Before long he entered the political arena, and served the state in the Lower House for six years (1827–1833) and in the Senate for four more (1833–1837), the last two of which he was president of the body. A brilliant career as a statesman lay before him, but he retired at the age of forty-one to accept the secretaryship of the newly created State Board of Education. Through that office, however, he was destined to elevate education not only in Massachusetts, but through all the Union.

At forty-one he retired from politics, to become secretary of the new Massachusetts Board of Education.

His Fitness for the Secretaryship of the State Board of Education

Horace Mann's equipment for this, his real work in life, will readily be perceived. By heredity and early training he was suffused with an interest in humanity and all phases of philanthropy. This manifested itself preëminently in his efforts in behalf of education, although he was always an ardent worker for the cause of charity, the kindly treatment of defectives and

He was ideally equipped for educational reform, and entered upon the office with devotion.

[1] The heterodoxy of Mann kept him from the ministry, the most natural agency for social reform in those times, but he seems to have gone into law with a similar spirit. "Never espouse the wrong side of a cause knowingly," he wrote later to a young lawyer, "and if unwittingly you find yourself on the wrong side, leap out as quickly as you would jump out of a vat of boiling brimstone." See Livingston's *American Portrait Gallery*, p. 196.

dependents,[1] temperance, anti-slavery, and all other forms of social improvement. An ardent belief in what he continually termed 'the improvability of man' is shown in all his college orations[2] and early public speeches, and his optimistic views were strengthened by reading the *Constitution of Man* by George Combe[3] and his later companionship with that high-minded exponent of phrenology. Mann's early potentiality had been further rendered actual and shaped by the best education available, by constant reading and thinking, and by experience in writing and speaking and in practicing and making law. He may well be judged oversanguine in his faith in knowledge and education as the means of social advancement, and it may be that he underestimated the inertia of custom, habit, and institutions; but just such an enthusiasm and consecration as his were essential for the prodigious reforms that were to be undertaken. He certainly possessed a remarkable combination of intelligence, courage, and experience for leadership in this direction. The law proposed for the new Board of Education numerous duties in the way of collecting and spreading information concerning the common schools and of making suggestions for the

[1] The greatest service in this direction was his aggressive advocacy of the establishment of the Insane Hospital at Worcester by the legislature.

[2] His graduation address at Brown was on *The Gradual Advancement of the Human Species in Dignity and Happiness*. [3] See footnote on p. 267.

improvement and extension of public education, but it provided no real powers. It was obvious that the permanence and influence of the Board would have to depend almost wholly upon the intelligence and force of character of its secretary, and the peculiar fitness of Mann can alone account for his selection. By reason of his efforts in behalf of educational reform, his persistent advocacy of the bill as a member of the legislature, and his undoubted merits as an educator, a schoolmaster named James G. Carter' would seem to have been the logical man for the secretaryship. The teachers of the state were bitterly disappointed that one outside their number should have been preferred, but it would now appear that the choice of a broadminded and philanthropic statesman was most wise. Mann, moreover, did not seek the place, and the surrender of a fairly lucrative practice and an assured career for the mere pittance and the uncertainty of the secretaryship was no small sacrifice. Yet his only hesitation was as to his qualifications for 'filling this high and responsible office,' and his zeal to 'adequately perform its duties.' Having accepted the responsibility, he wrote the governor that "so long as I hold this office, I devote myself to the supremest welfare of mankind upon earth," and, closing his law office, he made the memorable declaration:

"The interests of a client are small compared with the interests of the next generation.   Let the next generation, then, be my client."

His Labors in Reforming Education

His chief means of arousing the people and improving education were his campaigns through the state,

During the next twelve years, as secretary of the State Board, Horace Mann subserved the interests of his accepted client most faithfully. Educational ideals were in sad need of expansion and democratization, and school organization, curricula, and methods called for enlargement and a complete modernization. To awaken the people, the new secretary at once started upon an educational campaign through the state, and during each year of his tenure he made an annual circuit for this purpose. At first the reception given him was cold and spiritless; often after a hard journey he found but a handful of an audience, and upon one occasion he had even to sweep out the room himself and put it in order.[1] Keenly as he felt this want of appreciation, nothing could daunt him, and these annual visits gradually grew in interest and enthusiasm, and eventually he came to meet almost with ovations. Besides the regular trips, Mann held himself subject to calls from everywhere, within the state and out, for educational meetings, lectures, and addresses; and when, after seven years, teachers' institutes were introduced into

[1] It was at Pittsfield that he found this lack of preparation, and Governor Briggs assisted him in his janitorial duties. After a meeting in Northampton he declared: "I have found so large a mountain, there is danger that I shall break my own neck in trying to lift it."

Massachusetts, he constantly served as an efficient lecturer and instructor.

An even more effective means of disseminating Mann's reforms was found in the series of *Annual Reports* which he issued from the first, and in the publication of his *Common School Journal*, begun in the second year of his administration. The *Reports* were by law to give information concerning existing conditions and the progress made in the efficiency of public education each year, and to discuss the most approved organization, content, and methods for the common schools, in order to create and guide public opinion most intelligently. The material in these documents fills one thousand pages of Mann's collected *Works*. It exhibits the great benefits to the state and the individual of a public school training. While practically every educational topic of importance at the time is dealt with, his suggestions as a whole maintain a definite point of view and a connected body of practical doctrine. Sometimes they seem commonplace, but it must be remembered that they were not so then, and that the work of Mann did much to render them familiar. The last report contains a summary of what he had endeavored to accomplish and shows how all his criticism of the schools had been undertaken as a conscientious duty and with a full realization of what the consequences to himself would be. The *Reports* were frequently written

his *Annual Reports* to the State Board,

hastily and are sometimes poorly arranged, illogical, and exaggerated; but the style was always forceful and animated, and often fervid and eloquent. They are the most important and enduring of his writings, and will ever be regarded as educational classics. While addressed to the State Board, they were really intended for the citizens of Massachusetts in general, and their influence was felt far beyond the confines of the state. They vitally affected school conditions everywhere in New England, and were read with great interest in all parts of the United States, and even in Europe. An issue of eighteen thousand copies of one report was made for free distribution by act of the New York legislature, another was reprinted in Great Britain, and Germany translated and distributed editions of several.

his semi-
monthly
*Common
School
Journal,*

The *Common School Journal*, on the other hand, was issued semi-monthly and consisted of sixteen pages to each number. It was devoted to spreading information concerning school improvement, school law, and the proceedings of the State Board, and it urged upon school officials, parents, and children their duties toward health, morals, and intelligence. This publication, which was continued by Mann during the whole of his administration, laid him under the necessity of much writing himself and of securing contributions from other educators.

A medium somewhat akin to Mann's publications in the improvement of educational facilities was his general establishment of school libraries throughout Massa- *his encouragement of school libraries,* chusetts. This the reformer brought to pass in a large number of towns and school districts through a subsidy from the state. The first impulse was given these institutions in 1838; and while the enthusiasm for their creation and use lasted only five years, they were productive of an immense amount of good in creating a taste for proper reading and in democratizing education.

But probably the most permanent means of stimulating the revival and propagating the reforms led by Horace Mann was the foundation by Massachusetts of *and his establishment of the first three state normal schools.* the first public [1] normal schools in this country. A devoted friend of Mann [2] offered to donate ten thousand dollars for this purpose, in case the state would supply a like amount. This generous proposal was accepted by the legislature in 1838. It was decided to found three schools, so located that all parts of the

---

[1] James G. Carter established a short-lived normal institution in 1821 at Lancaster, Massachusetts, and the Rev. Samuel R. Hall conducted schools of this character in Vermont at Concord (1823–1830), Andover (1830–1837), and Plymouth (1837–1840); but the normals founded through Mann were the first under state auspices. See Dexter, *History of Education in the United States*, pp. 373 ff.

[2] Edmund Dwight, the member of the Board who had been most instrumental in bringing about the selection of Mann, and afterward assisted the work of the Board by gifts on several occasions and by supplements to Mann's salary, made this offer anonymously.

s

state might be equally served.[1] Although the name 'normal' was borrowed from France, the curriculum and methods of these institutions were largely influenced by those prevailing in the 'seminaries' for teachers in Prussia.[2] The course consisted in a review of the common branches from the teaching point of view, work in educational theory, and training in a practice school under supervision. Despite the hostility of conservatives, incompetent teachers, and sectarian dogmatists everywhere in the state, the schools, while not largely attended, were a great success from the start, and have been of immense service in raising the standard of teaching in Massachusetts and through New England.[3]

He lavished time and strength upon his work with totally inadequate compensation. The arduous and unremitting labors of Mann in instituting and promoting the various means of school reform must have made the greatest inroad upon his time and strength. His correspondence alone, in a day before the general use of stenography, typewriting, or even fountain pens, is estimated to have averaged thirty or forty letters a day. It is known that during his

---

[1] One school was to be in the northeast, another in the southeast, and the third in the less populated west. The first, located at Lexington, was afterward removed, first to West Newton, and then to Framingham; the second, started at Barre, was later taken to Westfield; but the third has always been situated at Bridgewater.

[2] See Graves, *History of Education during the Transition*, pp. 304 f.

[3] Much of the success and influence of the schools was due to the happy selection of the Rev. Cyrus Pierce for the first principalship.

entire incumbency his work extended over fifteen hours of each day, and that he was frequently afflicted with insomnia for weeks.[1] Moreover, through all this period, his income did not amount to a living wage. While his salary was at length raised from one thousand to fifteen hundred dollars, no allowance was made for running his office and but little for traveling expenses. He paid for many conventions and hundreds of copies of his *Reports* and *Journal* out of his own pocket. As a result, he was at times unable to purchase sufficiently nourishing food, and only the addition made to his salary by a wealthy admirer[2] kept him from want.

The Opposition of Conservative Politicians, Schoolmen, and Theologians

But the most trying obstacle that the great reformer had to contend with was the dense conservatism and bitter prejudices often animating people that he felt ought to have eagerly supported him in his herculean efforts. The Board and its secretary were for years violently assailed by sordid politicians, unprogressive schoolmen, and sectarian preachers. Attempts were early made in the legislature to abolish the Board of

He was bitterly opposed by all conservatives, —

politicians,

[1] When we remember that, as a consequence of overwork on the farm and in college, Mann was a 'lifelong invalid,' and that, owing to his official toil and want of sleep, his brain often 'flamed like a brush-pile on a distant heath in the wind,' the greatness of this conquest of mind over matter can be somewhat realized.   [2] See footnote 2 on p. 257.

Education or to have its duties and powers transferred to the governor and council, but after a fierce fight this type of opposition ceased.

Mann's controversy with the Boston schoolmasters was also sharp, but decisive. His *Seventh Annual Report* (1843) gave an account of his visit to foreign schools, especially those of Germany, and praised with great warmth the instruction without textbooks, the enthusiastic teachers, the absence of artificial rivalry, and the mild discipline in the Prussian system. The report did not stigmatize the conservatism of the Boston schools or bring them into comparison with those of Berlin, but the cap fitted only too well. The pedagogues were seriously disquieted, and proceeded to answer most savagely. Although not all the Boston teachers were opposed to the new order of things, the Principals' Association through a committee of thirty-one joined battle by issuing their *Remarks on the Seventh Annual Report of Hon. Horace Mann*. This was a pamphlet of one hundred and forty-four pages, which undertook to vindicate the historic educational system of Massachusetts, and to discredit the normal schools, libraries, methods, discipline, and other features of the new régime. The secretary straightway made a *Reply* of even greater length, and when they returned to the charge with a *Rejoinder*, he soon had an *Answer* ready. While much in Mann's pamphlets is unfair, weak in

Boston school principals,

argument, and unnecessarily severe, he had been un-
justly and deeply wounded, and in the main was felt
to be right. When the smoke of battle had cleared
away, it was seen that the leaders of the old order had
been completely routed and had wrought their own
destruction.[1]

A more insidious attack upon the broad-minded
reformer was that led by the ultra-orthodox. The old
schools of the Puritans with their dogmatic religious
teaching had been steadily fading away some time before
the new Board had been inaugurated, but the educational revival of Mann made this fact patent for the
first time. There was, in consequence, a tendency upon
the part of many conscientious but narrow people to
charge this disappearance to the reformer, whose liberal
attitude in religion was well known. Others took advantage of the popular clamor to vent upon Board and
secretary the spleen which for various reasons they had
accumulated against them. The assault, which cul-
minated with articles in the sectarian press and with
polemic sermons, was vigorously and successfully re-

and the ultra-orthodox.

---

[1] In fact, the prominence that this controversy gave him as the apostle
of reform was the making of Mann's reputation as a great educator.
We have, in consequence, been prone to forget, in our admiration of his
lofty character, strong determination, and great devotion that Mann was
not the only prominent educational leader of the times, and that men like
Carter were in the field long before him, and that Barnard served the
cause of the common schools for half a century afterward.

pelled by the secretary and others, including many of the more sensible orthodox people. Mann throughout the contest consistently maintained that the Bible should be read in the public schools, but without comment, and thus became the first educator of prominence to attempt an adjustment of the relations of state and church.

His After Life in Congress and at Antioch College

After a dozen years of service he retired and entered Congress, and later undertook the presidency of Antioch College.

In 1848 Mann resigned the secretaryship of the Board to enter Congress as an eloquent opponent to the extension of slavery.[1] While his subsequent life reveals the same high moral and philanthropic principles, his efforts after leaving the secretaryship do not especially concern us here. In 1853 he retired from active politics, and, in the hope of furthering certain advanced ideals that he held for higher education, he undertook the presidency of Antioch College at Yellow Springs, Ohio. The strain of building up the new institution, in addition to exhausting labors for many years, resulted in his death at the age of sixty-three. Until the end he reasoned earnestly with those he had summoned for counsel to his deathbed concerning 'truth, God, man, and duty.'

[1] After a most insistent demand on the part of his fellow-citizens, he entered Congress to fill out the unexpired term of John Quincy Adams, and was twice reëlected.

Mann's Educational Ideals

Thus passed a great soul whose influence would have been felt in any line of humanitarian endeavor, but whom circumstances led to perform his greatest services for the common schools. His general positions and specific recommendations concerning education may easily be gathered from his *Lectures, Reports,* and *Common School Journal.* A brief interpretative summary may give some idea of their purport and range. First and foremost he held that education should be universal and free. "I believe," he says, "in the existence of a great immortal, immutable principle of natural law, a principle of divine origin, clearly legible in the ways of Providence — the absolute right to an education of every human being that comes into the world." Girls should be trained as well as boys, and the poor should have the same opportunities as the rich. Public schools should afford education of such a quality that the wealthy would not patronize private institutions because of their superiority. And as Mann's reforms advanced, he took great pride in the fact that "more and more of the children of the Commonwealth are educated together under the same roof, on the same seats, with the same encouragement, rewards, punishments, and to the exclusion of adventitious and artificial distinctions."

Horace Mann believed in a universal and free education of the highest order.

The chief
aim of this
education
should be
moral char-
acter and
social effi-
ciency.

This universal education, however, should have as its chief aim moral character and social efficiency, and not mere erudition, culture, and accomplishments. "No amount of intellectual attainments," in Mann's judgment, "can afford a guaranty for the moral rectitude of the possessor." But while the public school should cultivate a moral and religious spirit, this could not be accomplished, he felt, by inculcating sectarian doctrines. The main objection urged to the private school system in his *First Report* was its tendency "to assimilate our modes of education to those of England, where Churchmen and Dissenters, each sect according to its creed, maintain separate schools in which children are taught from their tenderest years to wield the sword of polemics with fatal dexterity; and where the Gospel, instead of being a temple of peace, is converted into an armory of deadly weapons for social interminable warfare."

His Improvement of Material Equipment and of Methods

The material
equipment of
the schools
should re-
ceive careful
attention.

This practical reformer likewise gave much attention to the material side of education. He declared that school buildings should be well constructed and sanitary. This matter seemed to him so important that he wrote a special report upon the subject during his first year in office. He carefully discussed the proper plans for rooms, ventilation, lighting, seating, and other school-house features, and insisted that the inadequate and squalid conditions that were existing should be improved. In his *Fourth Report* also he considered many of the physical evils, especially those arising from pupils of all ages being in the same room. He found that in many cases this was the result of a multiplication of districts, and suggested union schools or consolidation as a remedy.

Instruction in the schools, he maintained, should be based upon scientific principles, and not authority and tradition. "Some teachers," said he, "will teach only from the books from which they themselves learned. This would create an hereditary descent of books, and the line would be immortal." And elsewhere he insists, "No one is so poor in resources for difficult emergencies as they may arise as he whose knowledge of methods is limited to the one by which he happened to be instructed." Pestalozzi's inductive method of teaching received his approval, for he felt that the pupils should be introduced at first-hand to the facts of the humanities and sciences. The work should be guided by able teachers, who had been trained in a normal school, and should be imparted in a spirit of mildness and kindness through an understanding of child nature. The teachers, who should be men as well as women, ought also to supplement their training and experience by frequent

The methods should be scientific, and the teachers should be trained.

He favored Pestalozzi's inductive method.

gathering in associations and institutes for mutual improvement and instruction.

His Emphasis upon Practical Studies

The studies should be adapted to practical needs.

In the matter of the studies to be pursued, Mann was inclined toward the practical, and held that educational values and the natural order were often neglected. In his *Sixth Report* he inquires: —

He overemphasized bookkeeping and physiology.

"Can any satisfactory ground be assigned why algebra, a branch which not one man in a thousand ever has occasion to use in the business of life, should be studied by more than twenty-three hundred pupils, and bookkeeping, which every man, even the day laborer, should understand, should be attended to by only a little more than half that number? Among farmers and roadmakers, why should geometry take the precedence of surveying; and among seekers after intellectual and moral truth, why should rhetoric have double the followers of logic?"

Similarly, he holds that of all subjects, except the rudiments, physiology should receive the most attention, and he writes an extended essay upon its use and value. He exaggerates the importance of this subject, possibly as a result of his devotion to phrenology;[1] and in his whole espousal of subjects that will prepare for concrete living, he seems very close to Spencer's test of "what knowledge is of the most worth."[2]

[1] See footnote on p. 267.   [2] See pp. 275 ff.

His Missionary Spirit and Its Achievements

In order that these various ideals might be realized, Mann insisted frequently that the state should spare no labor or expense. "A patriot," to his mind, "is known by the interest he takes in the common schools." But in a republic he felt that "education can never be attained without the consent of the whole people. Compulsion, even if it were desirable, is not an available instrument. Enlightenment, not coercion, is our resource. The nature of education must be explained." Or, as he declares elsewhere, "All improvements in the school suppose and require a corresponding and simultaneous improvement in public sentiment." It was such an elevation of ideals, effort, and expenditure that Horace Mann sought, and for which he began his great crusade. He was a man of action, and not a philosopher. He had no deep thoughts on the problems of education, and not much insight into its nature beyond a dim notion gained from phrenology [1] that there were certain great 'laws' in man's nature which would furnish a plan for education and moral reform. Most of his im-

Mann was not an educational philosopher, but an educational missionary.

[1] Phrenology was a reputable science in Mann's day. Such persons as Gall, Spurzheim, Combe, and, later, O. S. Fowler, show the standing of the subject then. Their theory of a localization of brain functions is now accepted by psychology in a general way, just as their contention that the amount of capacity in a given direction can be determined by measuring is generally rejected.

pulse was the direct result of his intense moral earnestness, to which his intellect was always subordinate. But it was just this characteristic that was needed to achieve the reforms he desired, and it alone accounts for the number of practical results accomplished by Mann.

His actual achievements cover a wide range. During the twelve years of his secretaryship the appropriations made for public education in Massachusetts were more than doubled. Through this rise in enthusiasm for public education, the proportion of expenditure for private schools in the state was reduced from seventy-five to thirty-six per cent of the total cost of schools. The salaries of masters in the public schools were raised sixty-two per cent, and, although the number of women teachers had grown fifty-four per cent, the average of their salaries was also increased fifty-one per cent. The school attendance enormously expanded both absolutely and relatively to the growth of population, and a full month was added to the average school year. Fifty new high schools were established, and the opportunities for secondary education, which had been fading for half a century, were once more opened. While the time for a full appreciation of skilled school superintendents had not yet arrived, Mann saw the value of careful supervision, and greatly increased its efficiency by making the compensation of visiting committees

His achievements were remarkable, — he doubled the appropriations for public education; he increased the number and salary of the teachers, the length of the school year, and the opportunities for secondary education; and brought about skilled supervision and professional training.

compulsory by law. He founded the first state normal schools, and insisted that teachers not only should have training and experience, but should constantly strive to raise the tone of the profession by attendance at teachers' institutes and county associations. Through him the idea of public school libraries was started and popularized.

Quite as marked was the improvement effected by Mann in the range and serviceability of the school studies, in textbooks, methods of teaching, and discipline. While not an educational theorist himself, he made practical and brought into use many of the contributions made to educational theory by others, and thereby anticipated many of the features of the so-called 'new' education. Through him was introduced the word method of reading in place of the uneconomical, artificial, and ineffective method of the alphabet. He advocated object methods and oral instruction. By him government and discipline were placed upon a rational basis. The connection between physical and mental health and development was often stressed in his writings.

He emphasized the word method of reading, object teaching and oral instruction, rational discipline, physical development, and other features of the 'new' education.

Effect of His Reforms upon Massachusetts and Other States

Thus through Horace Mann the people of Massachusetts renewed their faith in the common schools. While he was assisted by many progressive educators and

Through him the schools of Massachusetts have become organized; and the systems in other states have been centralized, and have caught his enthusiasm in all directions.

teachers of the times and a sympathetic Board of Education, it was under his immediate leadership that a practically unorganized set of schools, with diverse aims and methods, was welded into a well-ordered system with high ideals. The organization of state school administration under the control of a Board and secretary proved to be so efficient that until 1908 it remained in vogue in Massachusetts. Even now the only change is in the way of wider powers and centralization and the recognition of the responsibility and dignity of the executive officer by changing his title to 'state commissioner.'[1] But the influence of Horace Mann's work was not confined to Massachusetts. Through his reports, addresses, journal, and correspondence, the revival of common schools, which was going on in all the neighboring states, was heightened. Following the example of Massachusetts, the rest of New England began to centralize its educational administration, with a state board and secretary, as at first in Connecticut and in Maine, or with a single official known as a 'commissioner,' as in Rhode Island and New Hampshire, or 'superintendent of schools,' as later in Connecticut and in Vermont.[2] This organization and the suggestions of

[1] In 1908, after the state committee on the investigation of industrial education made its report, it was merged in the State Board, and provision was made for the appointment of a 'commissioner' with enlarged powers.

[2] In this connection we should not forget the marvelous work of *Henry Barnard* (1811–1900), who had a somewhat similar, though longer,

Mann proved most effective, and resulted in more systematic reports and great improvements in the training of teachers, material equipment, courses, textbooks, methods, and discipline throughout New England. Other states caught the enthusiasm along various lines. New York, which had been training its teachers through facilities in some of the academies, started a regular normal school, greatly improved its supervision, and finally separated the state superintendency of schools from the office of the secretary of state. Farther west, progress was made *pari passu* with the settlement of the country. Early in the secretaryship of Mann, Ohio established a state superintendency and an advanced set of school laws, and Michigan and other states made ample provision for their systems of common schools. A regular organization of the state schools, with a central authority of some sort, rapidly followed every-

career as an educator, and greatly supplemented Mann's work. He served as Secretary of the Board of School Commissioners in Connecticut (1838–1842), as School Commissioner of Rhode Island (1843–1849), and Superintendent of Schools for Connecticut (1850–1854). Later (1867–1870) he became the first United States Commissioner of Education. He expended a fortune in getting out the volumes of his monumental *American Journal of Education* (1855–1872), which has been the greatest mine of information in existence upon educational history, theory, and practice. Owing to the overshadowing importance attached to the great educational fight made by Mann, whose service for the common schools was, after all, comparatively brief, Henry Barnard has received altogether too little recognition.

where, and has continued as new states have come into existence.

Thus by the force of example the influence of Horace Mann has been felt in all parts of this country. Moreover, the personality of Mann and the improvements resulting from his work were recognized even in several states of Europe. Many articles and books upon this great educational statesman have been published by English, French, and Italian educators. His services have produced an effect both fundamental and widespread. They have proved a stimulus to foreign lands, and upon the United States they have made a lasting impression.

SUPPLEMENTARY READING [1]

I. Sources

*MANN, H. *Annual Reports of the Secretary of the Massachusetts Board of Education* (1838–1849), *Common School Journal*, and *Lectures on Education*.

MANN, MARY. *Lectures and Annual Reports on Education of Horace Mann* (Vol. II of Atkinson's *Life and Works of Horace Mann*).

II. Authorities

ATKINSON, W. P. *Life and Works of Horace Mann.* Five volumes.

BARNARD, H. *American Journal of Education.* Vol. V, pp. 611–645.

[1] A more complete bibliography by B. Pickman Mann can be found in the *Report of the United States Commissioner of Education*, 1895–1896, Vol. I, pp. 897–927.

BOWEN, F. *Mr. Mann and the Teachers of the Boston Schools* (*North American Review*, Vol. LX, pp. 224–246).

COMBE, G. *Education in America: State of Massachusetts* (*Edinburgh Review*, Vol. LXXIII, pp. 486–502).

*HARRIS, W. T. *Horace Mann* (*Educational Review*, Vol. XII, pp. 105–119).

*HINSDALE, B. A. *Horace Mann and the Common School Revival in the United States.*

HUBBELL, G. A. *Horace Mann; Educator, Patriot, and Reformer.*

KASSON, F. H. *Horace Mann* (*Education*, Vol. XII, pp. 36–43).

LANG, O. H. *Horace Mann, his Life and Work.*

MANN, MARY. *Life of Horace Mann.*

MARTIN, G. H. *Horace Mann and the Revival of Education in Massachusetts* (*Educational Review*, Vol. V, pp. 434–450).

MARTIN, G. H. *The Evolution of the Massachusetts Public School System.* Lect. IV.

*MAYO, A. D. *Horace Mann and the Great Revival of the American Common School*, 1830–1850 (*Report of the United States Commissioner of Education*, 1896–1897, Vol. I, pp. 715–767).

*PARKER, F. W. *Horace Mann* (*Educational Review*, Vol. XII, pp. 65–74).

*WINSHIP, A. E. *Horace Mann the Educator.*

CHAPTER XIV

HERBERT SPENCER AND THE RELATIVE VALUE
OF STUDIES

The natural
sciences were
greatly de-
veloped in
education
during the
latter half of
the nine-
teenth cen-
tury, and
the changed
attitude
was crystal-
lized by
Herbert
Spencer.

THE latter half of the nineteenth century witnessed a great development in the natural sciences and in the part they should play in the curricula of various educational institutions. At the beginning of this period, Greek and Latin had everywhere an almost unbroken monopoly in secondary and higher education, and stubbornly resisted the admission of any training in science; while, by the close of the century, not only was the power of the classical fetish greatly diminished, but a constant struggle and a complete revision of methods to maintain these subjects at all had become necessary. This general change of attitude grew largely out of the material development of the times, the increasing popularity of evolutionary doctrine, and the work of the educational reformers that had preceded. But while it was in the spirit of the times, it was first crystallized and defended by the English philosopher, Spencer.

Spencer's *Education* and Other Writings

Spencer was
reared amid
intellectual

Herbert Spencer (1820–1903) was the descendant of educators, and during all his youth was surrounded by intellectual and literary traditions. He never went to the university, possibly on account of the poor health from which he suffered all his life, but he engaged in a wide range of miscellaneous studies at home. He began early to read on natural science and mathematics, perform experiments and make inventions, and show remarkable ability in working out original problems. In his young manhood he wrote on economic and social subjects with great force and clearness. By the time he was thirty he had produced his *Social Statics*, in which he treats the evolution of society through natural laws, and during the next quarter of a century he devoted himself to a systematic development of his ideas. He elaborated and applied the laws of evolution to important questions in biology, psychology, ethics, politics, and sociology, and issued a monumental series of works. During his thirties he also worked out his ideas on education with much enthusiasm. His treatises were originally contributions to magazines, but in 1860 they were collected and published in book form as *Education, Intellectual, Moral,* and *Physical.*

traditions, and early showed an interest in science.

At forty he published his treatise on Education.

"What Knowledge Is of the Most Worth?"

Spencer did not read widely upon educational subjects, and his conceptions are largely his own, but in his *Education* he has apparently been affected by the atmosphere of the times, and has combined with his principles some of the ideas previously expressed by Rousseau, Pestalozzi, and Herbart. Of the four essays in the book, the first has been by far the most influential, and called forth the greatest amount of comment. This part of the work, which seeks to investigate *What Knowledge Is of Most Worth*, raises the whole question of the purpose of education, and is completely subversive of the old classical traditions. Spencer's argument runs as follows : [1] —

The first essay in this book is of most importance.

"In order of time decoration precedes dress. And in our universities and schools at the present moment the like antithesis holds. As the Orinoco Indian puts on his paint before leaving his hut, not with a view to any direct benefit, but because he would be ashamed to be seen without it ; so a boy's drilling in Latin and Greek is insisted on, not because of their intrinsic value, but that he may not be disgraced by being found ignorant of them. The comparative worths of different kinds of knowledge have been as yet scarcely even discussed — much less discussed in a methodic way with definite results. Before there can be a rational curriculum, we must decide which things it most concerns us to know. To this end, a measure of value is the first requisite. How to live ? — that is the essential question for us. Not how to live in the mere material sense only, but in the widest sense. To prepare us for complete living is the function which education has to discharge ; and the only rational mode of judging of any educational course is, to judge in what degree it discharges such function. Our first step must obviously be to classify, in the order of their importance, the leading kinds of activity which constitute human life. They may be arranged into : 1. Those activities which directly minister to self-preserva-

Here he argues that to decide What Knowledge Is of Most Worth, 'preparation for complete living' must be taken as a standard.

He then classifies the leading activities in life,

---

[1] In the quotation everything not essential to the argument is omitted.

tion; 2. Those activities which, by securing the necessaries of life, indirectly minister to self-preservation; 3. Those activities which have for their end the rearing and discipline of offspring; 4. Those activities which are involved in the maintenance of proper social and political relations; 5. Those miscellaneous activities which make up the leisure part of life, devoted to the gratification of the tastes and feelings. We do not mean that these divisions are definitely separable. We do not deny that they are intrinsically entangled with each other in such way that there can be no training for any that is not in some measure a training for all. Nor do we question that of each division there are portions more important than certain portions of the preceding divisions. But after making all qualifications, there still remain these broadly marked divisions; and these divisions subordinate one another in the foregoing order. The ideal of education is complete preparation in all these divisions. But failing this ideal, as in our phase of civilization every one must do more or less, the aim should be to maintain a due proportion between the degrees of preparation in each, greatest where the value is greatest, less where the value is less, least where the value is least."

The 'Sciences' Most Useful in All Life Activities

Applying this test, Spencer finds that a knowledge of the sciences is always most useful in life, and therefore of most worth. He considers each one of the five groups of activities and demonstrates the need of the knowledge of some science or sciences to guide it rightly. An acquaintance with physiology is necessary to the maintenance of health, and so for self-preservation; any form of industry or other means of indirect self-preservation

and holds that a knowledge of the sciences is a most valuable preparation for each.

will require some understanding of mathematics, physics, chemistry, biology, and sociology; to care for the physical, intellectual, and moral training of their children, parents should know the general principles of physiology, psychology, and ethics; a man is best fitted for citizenship through a knowledge of the science of history in its political, economic, and social aspects; and even the æsthetic or leisure side of life depends upon physiology, mechanics, and psychology as a basis for art, music, and poetry, and "science opens up realms of poetry where to the unscientific all is a blank." [1]

Besides the 'content' value, he also maintains that, on the side of 'discipline,' science trains the memory, judgment, and morals.

This argument for the sciences on the ground that their 'content' is so much superior for the activities of life would seem to be sufficient. But Spencer now shifts his whole point of view, and attempts to anticipate the defense of the classics on the score of 'formal discipline' by meeting them on their own ground. He admits that "besides its use for guidance in conduct, the acquisition of each order of facts has also its use as mental exercise, and its effects as a preparative for complete living have to be considered under both these heads." But he holds that by "the beautiful economy of Nature those classes of facts which are most useful for regulating conduct are best for strengthening the mental faculties, and the edu-

[1] Spencer even undertakes to show that a systematic knowledge of facts and the laws of science in the physical and psychological worlds is essential to the best æsthetic production and enjoyment.

cation of most value for guidance must at the same time be the education of most value for discipline." As evidence of this, he undertakes to show that science, like language, trains the memory, and in addition exercises the understanding; that it is superior to language in cultivating judgment; that, by fostering independence, perseverance, and sincerity, it furnishes a moral discipline; and even that science, "inasmuch as it generates a profound respect for, and an implicit faith in, those uniform laws which underlie all things," is the best discipline for religious culture. Hence, from the point of view of formal discipline and mental gymnastics, as well as of content and guidance, Spencer declares science, rather than language and literature, to be of most worth in education.

These educational conclusions of Spencer seem to involve a complete reversal of the Renaissance, and they certainly called for a loosening of the traditional hold of the classics upon England. Instead of Greek and Latin for 'culture' and 'discipline,' and an order of society where the few were educated for a life of elegant leisure, this English philosopher advocated the 'sciences' and a new scheme of life where every one should enjoy all advantages in the order of their relative value. We should, however, note the fallacy in his use of the word 'science.' With Spencer this term denotes the social, political, and moral sciences, as well as the physical and

Spencer is thus opposed to the classical traditions of the Renaissance, but does not, like Rousseau, deny the value of all knowledge that comes down from the past.

biological, and he really includes much that would properly come under the head of 'humanities' rather than 'science.' He is, however, fairly consistent in desiring material in the curriculum that will be of more service than the classics. While such a complete destruction of educational traditions strongly suggests Rousseau, Spencer's *Education* at least brought Rousseau's doctrine down to earth. It seems more like a reversion to Bacon and Locke, from whom the Swiss-French reformer probably got his start, and a return to England by way of the continent of the old revolutionary doctrines. It clearly cannot be considered Rousselian to the extent of denying the value of all knowledge that comes down from the past. His complaint lies rather against the monopoly of the traditional subjects and methods. "The attitude of the universities toward natural science," he protests elsewhere,[1] "has been that of contemptuous non-recognition. Collegiate authorities have long resisted, either actively or passively, the making of physiology, chemistry, geology, etc., subjects of examination."

His 'utilitarianism' includes moral as well as material, values.

Hence, Spencer cannot with propriety be stigmatized for his 'utilitarianism,' as has so frequently been done. His 'preparation for complete living' includes more than merely making a living and the material side of life, and the 'utilitarianism' with which he is charged contains

[1] *Social Statics*, p. 375.

the same underlying principle and may be equated with the 'practical' of Kant or the 'æsthetic' of Herbart. The 'science' with which he would replace the traditional humanistic studies contributes to moral values. It should elevate conduct, and make life pleasanter, nobler, and more effective.

His argument for the superiority of the sciences in disciplinary value, however, is unfortunate. There was no need of his accepting that point of view at all; and, in doing so, he shows that he is not altogether emancipated from tradition, and that he has not fully grasped the disciplinary claims of language, which he bases entirely upon memory training. He likewise begs the question in stating that nature is bound, as a matter of economy, to make the training that is best for guidance also the best for discipline. As a matter of fact, nothing is more uneconomical than nature, which always produces a superabundance, on the principle that much will necessarily be wasted.

His argument for the 'disciplinary' value of the sciences is, however, traditional, and his 'economy of nature' begs the question.

Essays upon 'Intellectual,' 'Moral,' and 'Physical Education'

The second essay in Spencer's work is entitled *Intellectual Education*, and deals largely with his ideas on method. In the first place, he insists, with Pestalozzi, "that education must conform to the natural process of evolution." He criticizes the methods of the time, and

In his *Intellectual Education* Spencer largely follows Pestalozzi's principles;

undertakes to state his guiding principles in logical order as follows: "1. In education we should proceed from the simple to the complex. 2. Our lessons ought to start from the concrete and end in the abstract. 3. The education of the child must accord both in mode and arrangement with the education of man considered historically. 4. In each branch of instruction we should proceed from the empirical to the rational. 5. The process of self-development should be encouraged to the fullest extent. 6. There is always a method productive of interest, and this is the method proved by all other tests to be the right one." These principles, which he exemplifies by applying them to various studies, are strikingly similar to some already formulated by Pestalozzi, Herbart, and Froebel.

in his *Moral Education* he holds to Rousseau's punishment by 'natural consequences'; and in his *Physical Education* he gives practical advice.

No greater originality is displayed in his essays upon *Moral Education* and *Physical Education*. In moral training, he criticizes the existing control by impulse, tradition, and harshness, and insists upon inhibition, repression, and elimination of the natural 'evil impulses' [1] as the 'guiding principle of moral education.' But while he does not agree with Rousseau that the child is by nature good,[1] he does indorse that writer's principle of punishing through 'natural consequences.' [2] In the

[1] In fact, despite his rejection of the old 'natural depravity' theory of the theologians, he holds, like Locke, a most unfavorable view of child-nature, and declares that "as the child's features resemble those of the savage, so, too, do his instincts."   [2] See p. 89.

matter of physical training, he holds that the first requisite to success in life is to be a good animal. He insists upon the preservation of health as a duty, and discusses most sensibly the proper food, clothing, exercise, and play for the boy and girl. Excessive study, he declares, should be avoided as fatal to happiness, and he would make but little use of set exercise, on the ground that it is artificial.

Influence of Spencer

Obviously, except for his definition of the aim of education and his test of the relative value of studies, there is little that is really original in Spencer. Yet his way of combining Rousseau, Pestalozzi, and other reformers was new, and gave a basis of solidity, practicality, and common sense to these educators. Herbert Spencer was probably one of the greatest minds the world has ever known. He was without question the one great English philosopher of the nineteenth century and the only educational writer of that country to make much impression upon the times. His treatise has been translated into thirteen languages and has influenced all parts of the civilized world. It has ever since given the sciences a standing that has assured them of complete recognition in the curriculum, and it is one of the most important works ever written in English.

Spencer thus worked out the relative value of studies and made a sensible combination of the theoretical reformers. He was the only English educationalist to make much impression on the nineteenth century.

SUPPLEMENTARY READING

I. Source

*Spencer, H.   *Education; Intellectual, Moral, and Physical.*

II. Authorities

*Compayré, G.   *History of Pedagogy.*   Pp. 538–556.

Compayré, G.   *Herbert Spencer and Scientific Education.*

Duncan, D.   *Life and Letters of Herbert Spencer.*

Gaupp, O.   *Herbert Spencer.*

*Harris, W. T.   *Herbert Spencer and What to Study* (*Educational Review*, Vol. XXIV, pp. 135–149).

Laurie, S. S.   *Herbert Spencer's Chapter on Moral Education* (*Educational Review*, Vol. IV, pp. 485–491).

*Laurie, S. S.   *Educational Opinion from the Renaissance.*   Chap. XVI.

Leitch, J.   *Practical Educationalists and their Systems.*

*Quick, R. H.   *Essays on Educational Reformers.*   Chap. XIX.

Royce, J.   *Herbert Spencer; an Estimate and a Review.*

INDEX

285

DATE DUE

MAY 5 '80	MAY 7 '80	OCT 08 '80	OCT 9 '80
FE 14 '85	FEB 18 '85		
GAYLORD			PRINTED IN U.S.A